The Corporate Investor Relations Function
A Survey

Research for Business Decisions, No. 30

Gunter Dufey, Series Editor
Professor of International Business and Finance
The University of Michigan

Other Titles in This Series

The Corporate Investor Relations Function

A Survey

by
Mollie Haley Wilson

RESEARCH PRESS

L 58.152
W 751

Text first published as a
typescript facsimile in 1978

Produced and distributed by
UMI Research Press
an imprint of
University Microfilms International
Ann Arbor, Michigan 48106

Library of Congress Cataloging in Publication Data

Wilson, Mollie Haley, 1942-
    The corporate investor relations function.

    (Research for business decisions ; no. 30)
    Bibliography: p.
    Includes index.
    1. Corporations—United States—Investor relations.
2. Disclosure of information (Securities law)—United
States.   I. Title. II. Series.
HD59.W54 1980   658.1'52   80-22459
ISBN 0-8357-1112-9

Contents

Acknowledgments

I wish to express appreciation to the many people who provided assistance and encouragement during my graduate career.

Dr. L.D. Belzung was among the first to encourage me in the graduate program. Dr. G.E. Kiser helped immeasurably, particularly in the questionnaire formulation stage of my research.

Mary Hirsch provided invaluable assistance with the program analysis of my data. Mike Heilman keypunched all my datacards—I would still be typing cards without his help.

I appreciate the support and encouragement of my friends and family during those years.

The person to whom I owe the most, however, is Dr. Robert E. Kennedy. Without his tolerance, encouragement, and support, I would never have completed the doctoral program.

This research effort, which is the culmination of my graduate studies, is dedicated to my mother.

1

Introduction

ROLES OF INVESTOR RELATIONS AND SECURITY ANALYSTS

Investors in the capital market continuously evaluate the securities of public corporations. To maintain the relative efficiency of this market, public corporations must disseminate information that is useful to investors in making investment decisions. This information dissemination can be an efficient mechanism for the capital market to allocate financial resources appropriately.

Corporate investor relations specialists and security analysts facilitate the flow and analysis of corporate information within the capital market. These functions must be performed in order to maintain the integrity of the capital market. One issue to be explored in this study is the extent to which these two functions are redundantly performed.

The investor relations function, as practiced by investor relations specialists, is of fairly recent origin and has become widespread among public corporations in the United States. The investor relations function is defined as the communications process, consisting of material information on which investors rely for investment decision-making. The growing and complex body of disclosure requirements and their enforcement has been initiated and governed largely by the Securities and Exchange Commission (SEC). Many large corporations now have increasing numbers of personnel to implement the investor relations function. This is illustrated by the growing membership in the National Investor Relations Institute (NIRI), an organization founded in 1970, whose membership today is overwhelmingly dominated by "in-house" investor relations specialists.

Security analysts constitute the principal "information network" through whom appropriate pricing decisions are made by investors in the capital markets. The 1980 Financial Analysts' Federation Membership Directory lists approximately 14,800 professional security analysts. Of these, approximately 6,000 Chartered Financial Analysts (CFA) also are listed in the latest (1978-1979) CFA Directory of Members.

CORPORATE INFORMATION TRENDS AND THE SEC

Concomitant with the rapid growth of investor relations specialists and security analysts is the ever-growing body of SEC regulations that have required a great increase in corporate disclosure to investors over the past decade. Such corporate disclosure is a major determinant of investment value in the capital market and generally is the basis upon which informed decision-making is made by investors. This study surveys opinions of investor relations (IR) specialists and chartered financial analysts (CFA) concerning the usefulness to investment decision-making of selected financial information, as well as the appropriateness of SEC requirements regarding the amount of corporate disclosure necessary to maintain the efficiency of the capital market.

Corporate disclosure falls into two broad classes of information: "hard" or historically oriented financial data such as long-term debt outstanding; and "soft" or future-oriented information such as sales and earnings forecasts. The "hard" information is subject to audit by public accounting firms; "soft" information disclosure is largely at the discretion of corporation management, subject to supervision by the SEC.

The SEC is now taking an active role in encouraging managements to disclose "soft" information. A decade ago, the SEC virtually forbade such disclosure. The attitudes of corporations, through their investor relations specialists, along with those of security analysts, on the question of "soft" information are also to be explored in this study.

THE MODERN INVESTMENT THEORY

During the past 15 years there has been a virtual revolution in academic financial thought, collectively referred to as "modern investment theory." These modern views, if accepted by the currently younger generation, will have profound implications for the investment practice in the future. Likewise, these views may have important implications for the roles of investor relations specialists and security analysts, as well as the information needs of investors generally, as enforced by the SEC.

Modern investment theory consists of two main developments. First is the efficient markets hypothesis, which states that: (1) securities prices reflect (discount) all known and knowable information; (2) investors cannot expect to earn above-normal returns; and (3) at any given time, securities are correctly priced (in equilibrium) in terms of their risk-return characteristics. The efficient markets hypothesis is in direct contrast to the conventional work of market technicians ("chartists") and security analysts.

The second development is the portfolio theory of Markowitz and its refinement into the capital asset pricing model (CAPM). This theory focus is on

portfolios, not individual securities; and it alters the way the risk-return characteristics of securities are viewed and priced. This theory implies that investors
should hold only "efficient portfolios," those diversified enough to eliminate
entirely all company (unsystematic) risks. Only market (systematic) risk
remains.

The capital asset pricing model asserts that only the "market portfolio"
(all companies weighted by their capitalizations), potentially combined with a
risk-free asset, should be held by investors. Accordingly, the search for above-
average investment returns will be fruitless. Obviously, this view constitutes a
further challenge to security analysts, as well as to the conventional practices of
portfolio managers. Indeed, the capital asset pricing model implies that the use
of "index funds" is the optimal way for large institutional funds to invest. The
CAPM and the efficient markets hypothesis are other issues to be explored in
this study.

STUDY PURPOSES AND JUSTIFICATION

The purpose of this study is to survey investor relations specialists and security
analysts regarding: (1) the perceived effectiveness of corporate investor relations
programs; (2) how investor relations specialists and security analysts rate each
other's performance; (3) attitudes toward selected "hard" and "soft" information disclosed by corporations that may be considered germane to investment
decision-making; and (4) attitudes toward selected ideas from modern investment theory as taught in graduate business schools.

It has been noted that the two groups interface with each other with
investor relations the "packager" and "sender" of corporate information and
security analysis the "receiver" and "evaluator." An analysis of the investor
relations-security analyst relation should consider the following: (1) how each
function rates the other's performance; (2) each group's attitude regarding the
relevance of selected corporate information for investment decision-making,
and (3) the ways in which these two functions may be affected by modern
investment theory as it becomes more widely known and accepted among
investment practitioners.

These three points warrant further discussion. On the first point, it is
important to recognize the two-way nature of this problem. While the investor
relations specialists are asked to evaluate their own programs (which may tend
to be self-serving), it is a check on the adequacy of these programs that they
are evaluated by security analysts. If investor relations specialists overrated
their own performance, it would imply that corporations are not effectively
communicating with analysts in terms of the latter's perceived needs. In any
case, the attitudes of security analysts can provide useful feedback to investor
relations specialists if they are, in fact, perceived as doing an unsatisfactory job.

Security analyst performance also is being measured by investor relations specialists. If security analysts are widely perceived as doing an unsatisfactory job, then corporations may choose to ignore them in favor of other information conduits, such as stockbrokers and portfolio managers. This would be unfortunate, since analysts constitute the principal information processing network in the capital market. The two-way communications problem between investor relations specialists and security analysts has not been explored in the academic literature. The exploration in this study is a first step in this neglected field of study.

On the second point, it is important for both groups surveyed to express their attitudes on the information content of selected corporate disclosures. "Hard" information must be disclosed by law (SEC), while "soft" information is left to the discretion of the company. The issue of "soft" information is substantially more controversial, and opposition by both corporations and security analysts probably would hamper the flow of this type of information to investors. However, if security analysts want this information, and it is perceived as useful in investment decision-making, pressure likely will build in time to cause corporations to reconsider their apparently negative attitudes on the issue.

On the third point, it would be a matter of academic interest to determine apparent acceptance or rejection of the main propositions and implications of modern investment theory. It seems likely that, if the current generation of finance students have become steeped in these new ideas, a major change will occur in the way that investment practices are conducted in the future. Current investment practitioners who strongly reject these ideas must retrain or reorient their job functions or become obsolete. Corporations and security analysts alike, in order to remain viable as good "communicators" and "evaluators," will need to be familiar with this new movement in finance theory.

RESEARCH DESIGN AND METHODOLOGY

The research design of this study follows the survey technique. Two specially designed and pre-tested questionnaires were sent to the two groups interfacing with each other in the capital market; namely, the investor relations specialists who are also members of the National Investor Relations Institute (NIRI), and security analysts who also hold the Chartered Financial Analyst (CFA) designation.

Data for this research project were collected by mailed questionnaire during the period June 26-July 28, 1978. The response rate of 30 per cent for NIRI members and 27 per cent for CFAs was considered adequate for statistical analysis.

The source for the NIRI names was the 1978 *NIRI Membership Directory*. Names of the CFA subjects were taken from the Institute of Chartered Financial

Analysts *Directory of Members (1977-1978).*

The NIRI is an organization of professional investor relations specialists, founded in 1969, with a membership of approximately 1,000. Its function is to disseminate corporate information on a timely and material basis to investment decision-makers. The NIRI asserts a claim to the highest standards and code of ethics for professional investor relations personnel. The entire membership of the NIRI (excluding external counseling firms) was surveyed.

The Institute of Chartered Financial Analysts (ICFA) is an organization of professional security analysts, founded in 1949, with approximately 6,000 members, whose function is to make investment recommendations based on analysis of corporate and other information. The CFAs, through their rigorous training and academic examinations, and through their high standards of conduct and code of ethics, represent "the cream of the crop" of all practicing security analysts. CFAs probably occupy the most influential position in capital markets in terms of analyzing, pricing, and recommending securities to investors.

The subset of the CFA population sampled consisted of those CFAs classified as being employed by brokerage and investment banking houses. They are the ones, more than any other CFA group, who produce research reports on corporations, who make frequent management contacts with corporations, and who make recommendations regarding corporate securities for investment portfolios. This group is characterized as sell-side analysts; they have the greatest familiarity with corporate investor relations programs and with the types and sources of corporate information requisite to valuation decisions.

The questionnaire to each group has four parts: Part I deals with each group's attitudes toward: (1) the objectives of corporate investor relations programs; (2) the success of these objectives; and (3) the activity level and success with respect to stock price performance of the investor relations programs. In particular, members of the NIRI group were also asked if its stocks are undervalued, fully priced, or overvalued; and, further, if they have formal, written investor relations policies.

Part II seeks information from the NIRI on the number of analysts following the NIRI-related companies, and how well these analysts do their jobs. Part II was slightly reworded for the CFAs regarding the number of companies they follow on a regular and irregular basis, and how well those companies perform in the supply of information so they can make informed judgments on corporate risks and values.

Parts I and II of the questionnaire were designed to be similar but not identical. In Part I each group assessed investor relations programs in terms of the perceived performance of such programs. In Part II each group assessed the other in terms of the quality of information disclosure of corporations that enabled security analysts to examine corporate risks and investment values. To this extent, the two groups face each other and evaluate each other.

Parts III and IV of the questionnaire are identical for both groups and are designed to elicit levels and comparative attitudes on matters of common interest or distaste to both groups.

Part III seeks opinions from both groups on the comparative merits for investment decision-making of disclosure, either required or encouraged by the SEC. Thus, questions are formulated regarding selected types of "hard" information (i.e., line of business reporting), "soft" information (sales and earnings forecasts by corporations), and information overkill when presumably the costs do not justify the benefits of additional disclosure.

Finally, Part IV addresses itself to modern investment theory, and seeks information from both groups about their opinions regarding new ideas being taught in graduate schools of business. Thus, questions are formulated with respect to the theory of random walks, the role of chartists, the implications of stock splits, the role of security analysts in efficient markets, the central concept (beta) in the capital asset pricing model, and the use of "index funds." Further, both groups were asked about their familiarity with, and influence of, modern investment theory on the performance of their jobs.

In most parts of the questionnaire, a five-point scale is used to compare their attitudes and opinions. In a few places, only a three-point scale is used. Space also is reserved for specific and individualized responses. It was discovered through pre-testing that the questionnaire takes about 10 minutes to complete. The researcher believes that the response rate was satisfactory because of the minimal time involved in completion of the questionnaire, and its interesting and relevant contents.

The methodology employed was to assemble and examine the responses, and to tabulate the percentage distributions on the scales employed. For example, the five-point scale would range from a requested response of "very poorly" to "very well" or of "strongly disagree" to "strongly agree." By inspection, one could examine the compiled results in terms of the principal cell, or combination of cells, to which the responses belong, and thus compare the answers about the comparative attitudes of the two groups being surveyed.

Since there was no a priori knowledge of the nature of the statistical distributions of the responses, it could not be concluded that the populations being surveyed (sampled) formed a normal distribution. For this reason, parametric statistics were not employed. The test statistic used was the nonparametric chi-square (x^2) test which, at a .05 level of statistical significance either accepted or rejected the hypothesis tested for each component of the questionnaire, which called for a scaled response to a question. Thus, where applicable, the hypothesis tested was:

H_0: The null hypothesis that there is no significant difference, at the .05 level of significance, between the responses of the two groups surveyed.

H_a: The hypothesis that there is a significant difference, at the .05 level of significance, between the responses of the two groups surveyed.

The chi-square values, the degree of freedom, and the probability coefficient for accepting or rejecting the hypothesis are shown in each table in Chapter 5. It is important to note that the chi-square test statistic applies quite well to Parts II and IV of the questionnaire, where identical questions are asked, but is limited in its application to certain components of Parts I and II, which asked somewhat different questions.

Finally, it should be noted that this research project, organized around the use of questionnaires, suffers from the usual limitations of the survey technique, and further, inferences and generalizations must be made with caution.

STUDY CHAPTER PLAN

The remainder of the study is divided into five chapters. Chapter 2 defines the investor relations function and reviews the limited literature on this subject. Chapter 2 also defines the security analyst function and selectively reviews the large body of literature. Further, the professionalization of both the investor relations and security analyst functions is examined. Chapter 2 is the theoretical background to Parts I and II of the questionnaire.

Chapter 3 explores the significance of corporate and financial information for investment decision-making and summarizes the nature and trend involved in "hard" and "soft" information, especially as administered by the SEC. The issue of information "overload" also is presented. Accordingly, Chapter 3 is the theoretical framework for Part III of the questionnaires.

Chapter 4 develops the confluence of ideas and academic research leading to the formulation of modern investment theory. It discusses the variant forms of the efficient markets hypothesis, the advent of the Markowitz mean-variance portfolio approach, and its later development of the capital asset pricing model. Chapter 4 is the theoretical framework for a view of the evolution and development of modern investment theory that is presented in Part IV of the questionnaire.

Chapter 5 contains a discussion of the research design, the sampling and data collection procedures, and the nonparametric methodology employed. The responses to the questionnaires are tabulated and evaluated.

Finally, Chapter 6 provides a summary and conclusion and some implications regarding the findings of this research project.

2

Investor Relations and Security Analyst Functions

DEFINITION OF INVESTOR RELATIONS FUNCTION AND REVIEW OF LITERATURE

In a competitive economy, public corporations engage in investor-oriented activities by disclosing to investors material information on their progress and outlook. This enables investors to make intelligent investment decisions about corporate securities; it also allows corporations to raise funds periodically from capital markets to finance expansion and liquidity needs. In the widest sense, investor relations is the performance of these management activities and disclosure to the investment public; it embraces any corporate act that might be germane to investors.

For purpose of this study, the following definition of investor relations is adopted:

> Investor relations is the communications function that links the public corporation with its relevant investment markets. It is the need and art of financial communication of relevant and timely information to all relevant investment markets so that investors can make intelligent risk-reward decisions concerning their prospective ownership position (buy-hold-sell).[1]

In the literature, the term "investor relations" usually is interchangeable with "financial public relations," "financial relations," "financial publicist," or "corporate communications."

The definition adopted here has four important reference points:

(1) how the corporation organizes itself to implement the investor relations function
(2) the various audiences with which the corporation communicates
(3) what information is conveyed to these audiences, and its "material" content, as defined by the SEC
(4) the media by which, and the communication channels through which, this information is transmitted in usable form

These four reference points will be more fully discussed in this chapter and in the review of literature for this chapter.

It is clear that investor relations is a top management responsibility (specifically a financial management responsibility) which cannot be delegated away. By tradition and law, top managements of public corporations must communicate, at least with their owners (shareholders). They usually choose to communicate with potential investors as well. Since 1933, the minimal standards for informing shareholders have been set by the SEC and by the various state securities commissions that enforce their respective securities acts, called "blue sky" laws.

In a research study published in 1967, the National Industrial Conference Board noted that:

> Certain common patterns of responsibility are found in virtually every company's investor relations efforts. For one thing, the chief executive officer is always personally involved to some extent, if only through his participation in the annual meeting; in some smaller companies, he oversees the total program. For another thing, the chief financial officer is always active, commonly having such duties as preparing financial statements for reports to shareholders and granting interviews to financial analysts. And the corporate secretary universally assumes some responsibility for investor relations—at a minimum, proxy preparation and shareholder record-keeping.
>
> In fact investors relations activities are of such a broad and diffuse nature that, in most companies, several members of top or near-top management are called upon to help.[2]

Further, the study states:

> The function is never considered unimportant, nor is it relegated to a middle management position. And many executives make the point that, whatever the title of the executive responsible, he must, if he is to be effective, have ready access to top management, understand corporate objectives, and be thoroughly familiar with corporate activities.[3]

Some recognition is devoted to investor relations in the "practical" literature pertaining to management practices and activities. However, very little time or attention is devoted to investor relations in the theoretical literature. For example, in the more abstract literature in financial management—which is where investor relations would be positioned organizationally—there are few concrete articles or references in textbooks to this important financial management function. To illustrate, J. Fred Weston delineates the financial management function as follows:

A.   Specific Finance Areas
    1.   Management of fund flows
        a.   Effective acquisition of funds
        b.   Efficient utilization of funds

      c.   Analysis of fund flows
      d.   Specification and monitoring of liquidity objectives or constraints
  2. Management of capital
      a.   Management of the financing mix
      b.   Utilization of capital budgeting concepts
      c.   Analysis of decisions and actions affecting values
      d.   Maximization of capital values

B. General Management Functions
  3. Management of information flows
      a.   Formulation of a system of accounts to guide resource allocation
      b.   Analysis of portfolio decisions
  4. Management of the planning and control process
      a.   Analysis to set standards
      b.   Formulation of alternatives, plans, and policies
      c.   Periodic review of performance in comparison with plant
      d.   Corrective actions and modification of plans
      e.   Incentives system to reward and penalize performance in order to realize the firm's full potentials[4]

Weston's enumeration, which is fairly typical in the academic literature on financial management, fails to mention communications at all. Investor relations is implied, at most, in "maximization of capital values" (A.2.d above). This is an oversight on the part of finance and management theories and it cannot be accounted for easily. Perhaps investor relations is simply taken for granted, or the reason for its omission may be that it is a relatively new field for academic study and has not yet received adequate attention. The latter is the more probable cause.

Since investor relations is a financial management function at the practical and organizational level, the financial executive is usually in charge, reporting directly to the president of the corporation (Tables 1 and 2).

Some large companies have entire departments to implement the investor relations function. In small public companies, investor relations may be perfomed informally by one or more persons. Large corporations often have professionally trained staffs of investor relations and public relations specialists whose credentials and professional ethics are tied to such external organizations as the NIRI and the PRSA (Public Relations Society of America). In small companies, the investor relations function may be shuffled from one department to another, depending upon who has the time for it. In any case, corporations spend billions of dollars annually on the investor relations function.

Table 1.   Executives in Charge of Investor Relations in 196 Companies

Functional Classification	Number of Executives
Financial executive	77
Public relations executive	23
Secretary or assistant	21
President	14
"Dual" executive (e.g., secretary/treasurer)	9
Chairman of the board	8
Assistant to the president	6
Executive vice-president	5
Investor relations manager (or equivalent)	4
Legal executive	3
Vice chairman of the board	1
Outside public relations firm	1
Shared by two or more executives	24
Total	196

Source: Lowell Laporte, *Investor Relations,* Studies in Business Policy, No. 124, The
     Conference Board, 1967, p. 49.

Table 2.   Position to Which Various Executives Report

Executive Responsible for Investor Relations	Bd. of Directors	Chrman. of the Bd.	Vice Chrman. of the Bd.	Pres.	Exec. V.P.	V.P. Fin.	V.P. Pub. Rel.
Chairman	9						
Vice Chairman	15						
President		2					
Assistant to the President		1		6			
Executive Vice-President		6		9			
Vice-President–Finance	1	2	1	24	2		
Treasurer	2	9		30	4	8	
Secretary		8		22	1	1	
VP–Public Relations	1			16	2	1	
Secretary/Treasurer		2	2	6			
Vice-President/Controller				3			
Director of Investor Relations					1		
General Counsel	1	1		2	1		2
Total	29	31	3	118	11	10	2

Source: Lowell Laporte, *Investor Relations*, Studies in Business Policy, No. 124, The Conference Board, 1967, p. 55.

There are a number of strictly financial audiences with whom the corporation communicates, each with slightly different perceptions and needs for information. These include:

1. Stockholders
2. Security analysts
3. Stockbrokers
4. Portfolio managers
5. Investment bankers
6. Market makers, if over-the-counter
7. The exchanges, if stock is listed
8. Institutional investors
9. Long-term lending institutions
10. Foreign investors
11. Employees, if an Employee Stock Option Trust (ESOT)
12. Financial media, for the general public (i.e., Wall Street Journal)
13. Government (the SEC)

More general audiences also interested in timely financial and investment information are:

1. The company's own internal organization
2. Customers
3. Competition
4. Suppliers
5. Unions

To reach these audiences, mailing lists and contact points must be prepared, implemented, and updated. This job can be time-consuming and expensive for the corporation and requires periodic screening of the lists to keep names current and relevant. Most corporations include far too many names and repetitions in their mailing lists and fail to update the lists to include the right people.

Next, what information should be conveyed to these investment audiences? This depends on the objectives of corporate disclosure as promulgated by such organizations as the SEC, the Exchanges, the American Institute of Certified Public Accountants (AICPA), and others. For example, the SEC Advisory Committee on Corporate Disclosure states that the objectives should be: "To assure the public availability in an efficient and reasonable manner on a timely basis of reliable, firm-oriented information material to informed investment, and corporate suffrage decision making."[5] This definition of objectives "represents a primary emphasis upon the informational role of disclosure"[6] and emphasizes the investor as the primary user of this information.

The New York Stock Exchange (NYSE) has adopted a similar position. It states that:

> A corporation whose stock is listed on the NYSE is expected to release quickly to the public any news or information which might reasonably be expected to materially affect the market for securities.[7]

Similarly, the NYSE states the objective as:

> Timely disclosure to the public and to the Exchange of information that may affect security values or influence investment decisions, and in which stockholders, the public and the Exchange have a warrantable interest.[8]

Investment theory and valuation models will not be discussed at this point, but it is clear that corporations must disclose any information which would affect "the market for securities" and "influence investment decisions." There is a very wide body of theoretical literature on this subject, as well as an equally large practical literature on how securities should be valued. Certainly there is still widespread disagreement on any appropriate valuation model by which investors are believed to make investment decisions. The SEC gives no clues as to how investors make investment decisions. Not surprisingly, the corporate community views with uncertainty the question of "relevant" and "material" information that "may affect security values or influence investment decisions,"[9] and so corporations disclose a great deal of corporation information which may turn out to be irrelevant for investment decision-making. Thus, corporations invoke the "safety first" rule. However, corporations are not entirely uniform in this practice; some disclose considerable information while others say as little as possible.

Corporations tend to disclose information on their corporate and financial backgrounds (history), on changes in variables affecting corporate developments (contemporary events), and, occasionally, on definite statements about their prospects and outlook (forecasts). All three dimensions—past, present, and future—could be expected to enter into investor decision-making. On the dimension of contemporary events, companies find it practical to comment, by press release, on changes relating to a wide variety of firm-oriented events. These generally include changes in:

1. Operating results and financial circumstances
2. Management and organization
3. Product innovation; new markets
4. Plant expansions; new technologies
5. Competition and industry
6. Impact of economic factors; government policies, new legislation

and many other changes, internal or external, that might have a bearing on how investors appraise security values

Finally, corporations communicate with their various audiences in the following ways:

1. Written reports
   a. Annual report and form 10-K report filed with the SEC; proxy materials
   b. Quarterly and interim reports, 10-Q and 8-K
   c. Press releases directly to the public and through the news media
   d. Research report to investors via security analysts and financial media (i.e., Wall Street Journal)
   e. Letters to inquiring parties
   f. Prospectus, if "going public" or "merging"
2. Personalized contacts
   a. Shareholders via the annual stockholders' meeting; also special stockholder meetings
   b. Information meetings with groups of security analysts, stock-brokers, investment bankers, and portfolio managers
   c. "One-on-one" contacts with analysts, brokers, investors through letters, phone calls, or in person

This scarcely exhausts the list; the channels of communication are numerous. As Ray Garrett, Jr., Chairman of the Securities and Exchange Commission in 1976, has noted, the whole problem of corporate communications is far from being fully resolved, even at the level of the SEC. He said:

> But we are still faced with the question that has puzzled the Commission for forty years. How do we get the information spread to the persons who need it in a form in which they can use it? We have made some progress in making the official forms or reports filed with us available. Copies in the form of microfiche can be read, and hard copies procured, both in Washington and in some of our regional offices. There is also a service for supplying these by mail upon request at a small charge. We should be able to improve this system shortly. But we will probably never be able to put the official Form 10-K, or the 10-Q's, or the 8-K's, in the hands of the ordinary investor or the ordinary registered representative discussing a purchase or sale with the ordinary investor with anything like the efficiency that is accomplished by the corporation's own annual report to shareholders. What should we do? We want completed accurate information spread abroad as widely as possible to be available to anybody interested in it and on the other hand we do not want to impose upon companies of all shapes and sizes unreasonable trouble and expense, and we don't want to impede the flow of communication from management to its shareholders.[10]

DEFINITION OF SECURITY ANALYST AND REVIEW OF LITERATURE

Security or financial analysis, in comparison with investor relations, has a long and venerable history. Its early beginnings, especially in relation to common stocks, can be traced to the turn of the century, when a considerable number of companies listed on the New York Stock Exchange. This development alone is said to constitute the change in the American economy from "industrial capitalism" to "financial capitalism."

In this early period, all securities, including common stocks, were analyzed primarily by bond criteria. Only bonds were thought to exemplify investments; common stocks were considered speculations. Irving Fisher broke with this position by arguing that while bonds (fixed income securities) are the appropriate investment in times of deflation, high grade common stocks (variable income securities) are appropriate in times of inflation.[11]

A considerable number of books and articles appearing during the 1920s that further broke with the traditional idea that bonds are preferable to common stocks as investment media. In 1924, E.L. Smith suggested that even during periods of deflation, common stocks are superior investments, due to the operation of compound interest. As Smith states:

> Over a period of years the principle value of a well diversified holding of common stocks of representative corporations in essential industries tends to increase in accordance with the operation of compound interest.[12]

The stock market crash of 1929 and the Great Depression of the 1930s caused the entire investment community to reexamine its theories and to move away from the exuberance and optimism of the 1920s. The Great Depression influenced the works of Benjamin Graham and David L. Dodd,[13] which led to revised criteria and procedures for the analysis of securities, with emphasis on such concepts as fundamental value, margin of safety, diversification, and other conservative methodology in the consideration of securities. Security analysis, as viewed today, was fathered by Graham and Dodd,[14] and this book has been the bible by which most security analysts have been trained for the past four decades. According to Graham and Dodd,

> The objectives of security analysis are twofold. First, it seeks to present the important facts regarding a stock or bond issue, in a manner most informing and useful to an actual or potential owner. Second, it seeks to reach dependable conclusions, based upon the facts and applicable standards, as to the safety and attractiveness of a given security at the current or an assumed price.[15]

They further state that the functions of security analysis are threefold. First is the descriptive function, marshalling "the important facts relating to an issue and presenting them in a coherent, readily intelligible manner."[16] Among others things, this means the ranking and evaluating of favorable and unfavorable factors that affect a given securities issue.

Second is the selective function, where the analyst must be prepared "to pass judgment on the merits of securities."[17] This is the advisory function and requires a buy-hold-sell strategy for an investor, with consideration given to that investor's risk aversion, psychological make-up, resources, and other factors. This stage of analysis incorporates the margin-of-safety concept, especially for common stocks, in which the analyst "attempts to value a common stock independently of its market price."[18] This leads to the important concept referred to as "intrinsic value" or "central value," which in relation to market price means a security is "undervalued," "overvalued," or "fully valued." These concepts are central to Graham and Dodd's analysis and are considered important in this study's survey effort (see Questionnaire for Investor Relations, Part I, Question 7; Part II). Further, it should be noted that modern investment theory (Chapter 4) takes a radical departure from the Graham and Dodd thesis.

Third, according to Graham and Dodd, is the critical function of security analysis, in which the analyst examines his own standards of conducted selection, corporate accounting methods, corporate policies, and other matters of concern to stock- and bond-holders.[19] These functions of security analysis have led Graham and Dodd to believe that the field can become a discipline, and that "security analysts [should] be given a professional standing by setting up a rating or certification generally similar to that of certified public accountants."[20] This has now been accomplished by the Chartered Financial Analyst (CFA) certification, which will be discussed later in this chapter. In a book used as complementary reading for the CFA exams, security or financial analysis is a term that covers "the entire function of securities investment management":

> A financial analyst thus is one who: (1) analyzes companies and industries and makes recommendations thereon, or (2) as a principal or advisor selects securities for purchase or sale in an investment portfolio to achieve the objectives of the fund, or (3) manages all or part of the organization responsible for those functions.[21]

The security analyst usually goes through a comprehensive and systematic effort to describe, analyze, and understand the relevant factors that affect the value of securities and give advice concerning the purchase of them. For example, in common stock analysis, he examines factors relating to: (1) macroeconomic environment; (2) industry and company factors; (3) financial analysis; and (4) valuation of the corporate securities. An analytic framework for security analysts, representative of that used by practitioners and by professors of investments to illustrate security analysis, is presented in Table 3.

The security analyst is a key factor in the investment process, which is itself vital to the efficient allocation of resources in the American economy. As William C. Norby notes:

> The financial analyst plays a key role in this capital allocation process. As a security analyst he studies and selects industries and companies, interacting with the economist who provides the general economic framework. As a portfolio manager he integrates the work of the economist on the outlook for business and the financial markets with the securities recommendations of the analyst to make portfolio selections. These roles are interdependent; each contributes a necessary element to the investment decision.[22]

With the advent of institutional investors, who tend to dominate the securities markets today, the security analyst typically is a part of a multi-purpose investment organization that relies, on one end, on the professional economist, and on the other, the professional portfolio manager. Thus, the security analyst operates as a critical input to the investment process and to investor portfolios. The security analyst may be an industry specialist, a market technician, a generalist, or a portfolio manager. He may operate on the "sell side," representing research by brokerage firms, with the research sold (utilized) for "hard" or "soft" dollars by intermediaries or end-users (portfolio managers). The security analyst may, on the other hand, operate on the "buy side," repre-senting institutional investors who examine a variety of sell side recommenda-tions for inclusion in portfolios. The investment decision process, where the security analyst makes inputs through industry studies and company analyses, may be modeled as shown in Table 4.

An important part of this study is the interfacing of the investor relations and security analyst functions, and the importance of each group to the other. Richard M. Brodrick sees the situation this way:

> The interesting thing, however, is that investor relations is really only one side of a coin, and the coin itself is somewhat like an electrical conduit. The other side is the financial analyst. Each is trying to transmit, to the very best of his ability, the in-formation from the company (source of power or information) to the entire invest-ment community (end user).[23]

William Chatlos views the importance of security analysts as follows:

> It has been estimated that 80 percent of the transactions on the major stock exchanges are made on broker's recommendations that originate with brokerage firms' security analysts. While the status of a company's securities will not be solely dependent on the reactions of security analysts, analysts are an extremely important source of information for investors that cannot be ignored. Companies become particularly aware of analysts' potential power over the securities market when they watch in horror as their stock price plummets after a negative research report is released.[24]

Table 3.   Analytical Framework for Security Analysis

---

1. Environmental
   Economic growth and development
   Business cycles
   Money markets/prices
   Government activities and political risks
   International situation
   Social and demographic
   Stock market/investor confidence

2. Industry
   Product character and demand analysis
   Growth and development of industry
   R/D/E–innovation
   Economic structure/market power

3. Company
   History
   Product mix and differentiation
   Capacity utilization and expansion
   R and D programming
   Competitive position in industry
   Management factors
   Shareholders data

4. Financial analysis
   Quality of audit/footnotes
   Adjustments
   Spread sheets
   Ratio analysis*
   Financial profile

5. Pricing/Timing
   Concepts/measures of risk
   Past earning/dividend record
   Comparative PERs
   Timing devices (technical analysis)
   B/H/S actions

* Ratio Checkpoints:

1. Liquidity/WC/CF	4. Turnover	7. PERS–Comparative
2. Capital structure	5. Dividend/Yield	8. Quality of earnings
3. Operating efficiency	6. Bonds/Coverage	Stability
		Growth

Source: Robert E. Kennedy, Instruction Notes, University of Arkansas, Portfolio Management Class.

William H. Beaver regards the apparent significance of security analysts as an "informal information network" whose competition within the investment community has the probable effect of leading to efficiently priced securities (an axiom of the Efficient Markets Hypothesis in modern investment theory; see Chapter 4). Beaver says:

> The existence of financial and information intermediaries is undeniable. By recent estimates there are over 14,000 financial analysts. However, the precise role they play in the investment process is unclear. Management has incentives to provide information to analysts, and analysts have incentives to seek out and to disseminate such information. This informal information network appears to be enormous. It was reported that J.C. Penney logged in over 1,000 interviews with analysts in one year. This does not appear to be unusual for a company of J.C. Penney's size. In fact, this informal information network may be the mechanism which permits security prices to promptly reflect a broad information set. In other words, the competition among analysts for disclosures and for the interpretation of disclosures results in security prices that reflect a broad set of information. Statements of legislative intent at the time of the enactment of the securities acts indicate that at least some were relying upon the competition within the professional investment community to interpret the SEC filings and to effect an "efficiently" determined market price.[25]

INVESTOR RELATIONS SPECIALIST AND SECURITY ANALYST PROFESSIONALIZATION

Professionalization of the investor relations specialist and security analyst has made great progress in academic background, expertise and experience, knowledge required, and codes of ethics, which relate to professional status. Security analysts, by becoming Chartered Financial Analysts (CFA) and affiliating with the Institute of Chartered Financial Analysts (ICFA), are exposed to more stringent professional requirements than investor relations specialists. Major progress has been achieved in the investor relations area, however, through the generally high executive positions they hold with corporations, and affiliation with the National Investor Relations Institute (NIRI). Central to the purpose of this study is the fact that one begins with two professionally trained groups who occupy central positions in the capital market.

INVESTOR RELATIONS SPECIALIST PROFILE AND PROFESSIONALIZATION

There are approximately 1,000 professionals (as of July, 1980) who are members of the NIRI; about 200 of them represent outside consulting investor relations firms and 800 are in-house executives with corporations. Only the in-house personnel are of concern to this study. The NIRI Membership Directory

Table 4.   The Investment Decision Process

Information for Investment Decisions	Policy Decisions	Portfolio Decisions
Interest Rate Projections	Economic and Market Environment	Account Objectives Risk and Return
Profit Estimates Earnings of Market Averages Multiples and Values of Market Averages	Objectives for Types of Portfolios	Security Selection
Economic Projections – Long and Short Term		
Industry Studies Company Analyses	Portfolio Diversification Asset Selection Fixed-Equity Ratio Industry Weights	Performance Measurement

Source: Edmund A. Mennis, "An Integrated Approach to Portfolio Management," *Financial Analysts Handbook*, Vol. 1 Homewood, Ill.: Dow Jones-Irwin, 1975 , p. 1208.

indicates that most of the Fortune 500 companies are represented by in-house investor relations specialists.

In the fall of 1973, a special survey of NIRI members was conducted jointly by the NIRI and the Opinion Research Corporation. A follow-up survey was completed in July, 1979, and where the questions were the same, the 1979 results are used. Results of both surveys are interesting in terms of the professional status and achievements of NIRI members. Some of these findings are presented in the paragraphs and tables that follow.

Ninety-six per cent hold college degrees, and 40 per cent hold advanced degrees. Ninety-seven per cent earned more than $20,000 annually, and 64 per cent earned more than $40,000. Even given an inflation adjustment, these salaries are substantially higher in real terms than in 1973. In terms of their qualification and experience, 21 per cent came out of public relations; 59 per cent out of finance, and 7 per cent out of journalism; several other professional fields were also mentioned.[26] (Because of multiple listings, the survey results on this point exceeded 100 per cent.)

Forty-six per cent of those surveyed have been engaged in investor relations activities for less than 5 years. Forty-seven per cent have 6-15 years of experience, and 7 per cent have over 15 years. Forty-two per cent have been employed by their present company for less than 5 years, 23 per cent for 6-10 years, 11 per cent for 11-15 years, and 24 per cent for over 15 years.[27]

Organizationally, the 1973 survey of investor relations specialists showed that 59 per cent report to top management (presidents and senior vice-presidents), while 31 per cent report to the vice president level. In a similarly formulated question—"How many organization levels are between you and the chief executive?"—41 per cent said "No levels; I report directly to him," while 44 per cent said, "One level; my boss reports to the chief executive." One can conclude from these results that investor relations specialists generally hold important executive positions. Further, the investor relations function of the majority of corporations is centralized within one department (54 per cent), whereas it is scattered between departments (45 per cent) in the remaining cases surveyed. In terms of achieving their company's investor relations goals, 45 per cent said "Yes," and 45 per cent said "No." It will be interesting to compare this result with the Investor Relations Questionnaire, Questions No. 1 and No. 2.[28]

In the 1973 study, 76 per cent of NIRI members surveyed felt that membership in NIRI was valuable. Sixty-seven per cent found the national meetings to be instructive and useful. Sixty-nine per cent were especially interested in NIRI's emphasis on "building professionalism, status, and ethics."[29]

Some further facts on the professionalization trend of the NIRI are in order. First, the NIRI was founded in 1969, with the following objectives:

Table 5.   Education and Income

Education	Per Cent
BS/BA	51
MS/MBA	35
Ph.D.	2
LLB/LLD	3
No degree	4
Income	
Under $15,000	1
$15,000–$19,999	2
$20,000–$29,999	29
$30,000–$39,999	24
$40,000–$49,999	22
$50,000–$74,999	27
$75,000 or more	15

Source: National Investor Relations Institute, *A Perspective on Investor Relations.* Washington, D.C.: NIRI, 1979, pp. 14-15.

Table 6.   Areas of Primary Expertise

Expertise	Per Cent
Finance	59
Accounting	19
Public Relations	21
Journalism	7
Other	1

Other areas mentioned most often were:

> Advertising
>
> Employee Relations
>
> Engineering
>
> Corporate Planning
>
> Marketing

Source: National Investor Relations Institute, *A Perspective on Investor Relations,* Washington, D.C., NIRI, 1979, p. 9.

Table 7.   Years in Investor Relations Activities

Experience	Per Cent
Less than one year	6
1-5 years	40
6-10 years	33
11-15 years	14
16-20 years	4
Over 20 years	3

Source: National Investor Relations Institute, *A Perspective on Investor Relations,"* Washington, D.C.: NIRI, 1979, p. 4.

Table 8.   Value of NIRI Membership

Response	Per Cent
Very valuable	23
Fairly valuable	53
Not very valuable	17
No opinion	7

Source: National Investor Relations Institute, *A Broad-Based Study of the Investor Relations Profession.* Washington, D.C.: NIRI, 1974, p. 51.

Table 9.   Person to Whom You Report

Title	Per Cent
President	42
Senior Vice President	17
Vice President of Finance	15
Vice President	6
Treasurer	5
Vice President of Communications and Public Relations	5
Director of Public Relations	3
Other Officer	2
Director of Communications	1
Other Directors	1
Director of Investor Relations	1

Source: National Investor Relations Institute, *A Broad-Based Study of the Investor Relations Profession.* Washington, D.C.: NIRI, 1974, p. 8.

Table 10.   Organizational Levels

How many organization levels are between
you and the chief executive?

Levels	Per Cent
No levels, I report directly to him	41
1 level, my boss reports to the chief executive	44
2 levels	12
3 levels	1
4 levels	2

Source: National Investor Relations Institute, *A Broad-Based Study of the Investor Rela-tions Profession.* Washington, D.C.: NIRI, 1974, p. 9.

Table 11.   Achievement of Goals

Has investor relations with your company achieved
the goals or objectives established for it?

Goals Achieved	Per Cent
Yes	45
No	45
Half and half	3
No answer	7

Source: National Investor Relations Institute, *A Broad-Based Study of the Investor Rela-tions Profession.* Washington, D.C.: NIRI, 1974, p. 47.

To build a strong, attractive investment market by assuring equitable opportunities for every investor.

To work for better communications among corporate management, shareowners and the investing public.

To improve the techniques of investor relations through research, education and publication.

To encourage high ethical and professional standards in the investor relations function in corporate management.

To provide a forum for its members to present their views, to share experiences, to create and test investor relations policies, and to broaden the understanding of investor relations matters.

To serve as the representative voice and counselor—on behalf of its members—to Federal and State legislative bodies and executive agencies and to other interested organizations.[30]

Second, its code of ethics is stated as follows:

I. An investor relations practitioner should assist in maintaining the integrity and competency of investor relations.

II. An investor relations practitioner should assist in preventing the unethical or improper practice of investor relations.

III. An investor relations practitioner should preserve the properly confidential information of an employer or client.

IV. An investor relations practitioner should exercise independent professional judgment on behalf of an employer or client.

V. An investor relations practitioner will keep himself abreast of the affairs of his company or client and the laws and regulations affecting him and the practice of investor relations so that he will discharge his responsibilities competently.

VI. An investor relations practitioner should recognize his obligation to continually assist in maintaining and improving the free and fair access of individuals to a healthy securities market.

VII. An investor relations practitioner should avoid even the appearance of professional impropriety.[31]

Third, the NIRI sponsors a number of programs, societies, conferences, publications and the like to encourage professional training and participation. These are outlined as follows:

NIRI presents an annual educational seminar and encourages its chapters to carry on continuing programs of information and training in investor relations practices.

NIRI holds an annual national conference featuring timely presentations and discussions of issues and problems of interest to the legislative and executive agencies of government and the investment community.

NIRI encourages the organization of local chapters in major business centers. (Chapters are now active in the Boston, Chicago, Cleveland, Dallas, Detroit, Houston, Los Angeles, Milwaukee, Minneapolis/St. Paul, New York, Pacific Northwest, Philadelphia, Pittsburgh and San Francisco areas.)

NIRI publishes "IR Update," a newsletter containing reports on current developments of interest to investor relations officers, summaries of important papers or publications in the field, plans and programs of NIRI meetings, chapter activities, personal items, placement opportunities, etc.

NIRI maintains and cultivates a mutually helpful relationship with governmental agencies and leaders concerned with investor relations.

NIRI seeks opportunities to disseminate its views and policies by participating in public discussions and testifying before official agencies. It also provides a library, bibliographic and information service in the field of investor relations.[32]

In summary, the NIRI and its membership have made substantial progress in achieving its professional aims since its formation in 1969.

Further, the purpose of discussing in this study the professionalization of the investor relations specialist through membership in the National Investor Relations Institute (NIRI) is that: (1) most of the corporate executives implementing the investor relations functions among larger corporations are members of the NIRI, rather than other organizations that claim an interest in investor relations, such as the Public Relations Society of America (PRSA); (2) NIRI has an established plan and code of ethics for professionalization of its membership, whereas the other organizations do not meet these high standards of training and ethics; (3) this group is widely accepted as the dominant executive group in the implementation of investor relations policy. No other group, with these professional credentials, could be found for the purposes of this study.

SECURITY ANALYST PROFESSIONALIZATION: CHARTERED FINANCIAL ANALYST

The parent organization of the security analyst is the Financial Analyst Federation. Currently, 14,800 security analysts are listed in the 1979-1980 Supplement to the 1978 Membership Directory. There are 48 constituent societies in the major financial centers through the United States and Canada. It is considered one of the world's most influential organizations, and it is a forum before which SEC Commissioners, presidential candidates, and other important luminaries often give speeches. All public corporations wish to make investor relations appearances before the constituent societies, especially the New York Society of Security Analysts (the most prestigious of all societies and the highest recognition given in investor relations activities).

Professionalization of the security analyst has come with the advent of the Institute of Chartered Financial Analysts (ICFA) in 1959, which is associated with the Financial Analysts Federation (FAF). According to the ICFA Supplement to the Directory of Members (1979-1980), there are 6,011 CFAs, with over 2,000 candidates currently registered in the Study Program (for the CFA exams). There are age, experience, academic, and examination requirements in order to gain the CFA professional designation. The designation itself is national in scope, in connection with the institute headquarters at the University of Virginia, whereas, for example, the CPA degree for accountants is state-oriented in terms of its recognition and examinations.

The CFA profile is given in Tables 12, 13, 14, and 15. For purposes of this study, it is important to know that the CFAs surveyed come from the "Brokerage and Investment Banking" group of the industry classification (Table 12). When this study was made, these numbered 1,107, or approximately 25 per cent of total CFAs. This group represents the sell-side security analyst, whose job is to do creative and personalized research on the (1) analysis of companies and industries, (2) pricing of securities, and (3) recommendations to buy-hold-sell. Most of the remaining CFAs (those who were not surveyed) are buy-side security analysts, who depend for the most part on the research input from the sell-side analyst. It is consequently the sell-side analysts who are most familiar with companies and their investor relations programs and who can make the most knowledgeable assessments of the quality and aggressiveness of investor relations programs. The sell-side analysts have direct contact with the investor relations specialists and are the immediate demanders of corporate information. Clearly, they occupy a central position in the capital market. It is for this reason that this relatively small, but highly professional group is in the most strategic position to evaluate corporate investor relations programs, as questioned in Parts I and II of the questionnaire.

Toward the professionalization of the CFA, the objectives of the ICFA are:

To foster high standards of education and professional development in financial analysis.

To conduct and foster programs of research, study, discussion, and publishing which improve the practice of financial analysis.

Table 12:   CFA Profile: By Industry Classification

Industry Classification	Number of CFAs
Brokerage and investment banking	1265
Investment companies	358
Investment counselor	1027
Corporate financial executive	115
Trust companies and trust department of commercial banks	1218
Banking	177
Endowment funds, foundations, estates, pension funds, and other private funds	220
Insurance companies	616
Colleges and universities	96
Financial publisher	42
Public agencies	45
Financial consulting firms	104
Other	171

Source: Institute of Chartered Financial Analysts, *1979-1980 Supplement to 1977-1978 Directory of Members.* Charlottesville, Va.: ICFA, 1979, p. 10.

Table 13.   CFA Profile: By Degrees and Professional Designation

Degree and Professional Classification	Number of CFAs
Bachelors	1747
Masters	3289
Doctorates	161
Law graduates	93
CPA and C.A.	42
C.L.U.	8
C.P.C.U.	3
C.D.P.	1

Source: Institute of Chartered Financial Analysts, *1979-1980 Supplement to 1977-1978 Directory of Members.* Charlottesville, Va.: ICFA, 1979. p. 10.

Table 14.   CFA Profile: By Age Groups

Age Group	Number of CFAs
30 and under	233
31-35 years	1137
36-40 years	1274
41-45 years	987
46-50 years	746
51-55 years	434
56-60 years	231
61-65 years	188
Over 65	224

Source: Institute of Chartered Financial Analysts, *1979-1980 Supplement to 1977-1978 Directory of Members.* Charlottesville, Va.: ICFA, 1979, p. 11.

Table 15.   CFA Profile: By Sex

Sex	Number of CFAs
Male	5125
Female	329

Source: Institute of Chartered Financial Analysis, *1979-1980 Supplement to 1977-1978 Directory of Members.* Charlottesville, Va.: ICFA, 1979, p. 11.

To administer a study and examination program in financial analysis for C.F.A. candidates which guides analysts in mastering a professional body of knowledge, and in developing analytical skills, and which tests analysts for a reasonable level of competency.

To award the professional designation, Chartered Financial Analyst (C.F.A.), to persons who meet stipulated standards of competency and standards of conduct for the professional practice of financial analysis; and to permit persons to retain the C.F.A. designation who continue to meet stipulated standards.

To sponsor and enforce a Code of Ethics and Standards of Professional Conduct.[33]

The ICFA Code of Ethics is quoted as follows:

WHEREAS, the profession of financial analysis has evolved because of the increasing public need for competent, objective and trustworthy advice with regard to investments and financial management; and

WHEREAS, The Institute of Chartered Financial Analysts was organized to establish educational standards in the field of financial analysis, to conduct examinations of financial analysts and to award the professional designation of Chartered Financial Analyst, among other objectives; and

WHEREAS, despite a wide diversity of interest among analysts employed by banks, brokers and security dealers, investment advisory organizations, financial relations counselors, insurance companies, investment companies, investment trusts, pension trusts and other institutional investors and corporate bodies, there are nevertheless certain fundamental standards of conduct which should be common to all engaged in the profession of financial analysis and accepted and maintained by them; and

WHEREAS, the Institute of Chartered Financial Analysts adopted a Code of Ethics on March 14, 1964; and

WHEREAS, it is now deemed appropriate to make certain amendments to this Code:

NOW, THEREFORE, The Institute of Chartered Financial Analysts hereby adopts the following Code of Ethics and Standards of Professional Conduct:

A Chartered Financial Analyst should conduct himself with integrity and dignity and encourage such conduct by others in the profession.

A Chartered Financial Analyst should conduct himself and encourage the practice of financial analysis in a manner that would reflect credit on himself and on the profession.

A Chartered Financial Analyst should act with competence and strive to maintain and improve his competence and that of others in the profession.

A Chartered Financial Analyst should use proper care and exercise independent professional judgment.[34]

There are stringent examination requirements to gain the CFA designation. According to Norby, "The C.F.A. designation connotes the achievement in mastery of the body of knowledge of financial analysis and a commitment of high standards of professional conduct."[35] Three comprehensive exams, spaced over not less than three years, call for intensive knowledge of accounting, economics, financial analysis, portfolio management, and ethical standards.

Exam I emphasizes principles and techniques; Exam II emphasizes analytical use of techniques; and Exam III focuses on policy applications and ethical standards.

Candidacy examinations for the CFA designation were first offered in 1963, allowing certain people to be "grandfathered in" during the early years, thus taking less than three examinations. CFAs granted by year are shown in Table 16.

In the questionnaire sent to CFAs, selected profile information was sought on their titles, date the CFA was awarded, and academic credentials (Part I, CFA Questions 1, 2, 3). The main purpose of these questions is the control factor, confirming that those in the surveyed group are, in fact (1) CFAs, (2) sell-side analysts. The significance in this study of selecting sell-side CFAs for the survey is that they are accepted as the elite of professionally trained security analysis whose specialty is the financial analysis of corporate risks and investment values.

CRITERIA FOR SUCCESSFUL INVESTOR RELATIONS PROGRAM

One strong indication that security analysts and CFAs are interested in investor relations programs of corporations is the creation by the Financial Analysts Federation (FAF) of the Corporate Information Committee (CIC), whose central objective "is to encourage continuing improvement in the investor-related communications efforts of corporations."[36]

In the 1976 reporting period, the CIC sponsored 23 industry subcommittees, consisting of 186 analysts, who appraised the merits of the Communications Program of 590 corporations. The parent CIC Committee then reviewed the subcommittee reports and recommendations and gave "Awards for Excellence" to 38 companies in 20 industries. Winning companies included Ford, Citicorp, Sperry Rand, G.E., Murphy Oil, Dayton Hudson, Inland Steel, ATT, and 30 others.

A comprehensive set of criteria promulgated by the CIC is involved in the evaluation of a corporation's communications efforts. Taken as a document, it would be useful as a guideline to practicing investor relations specialists;

Table 16.   Year and Number of Charters Awarded

Year	No. of Charters	Year	No. of Charters	Year	No. of Charters
1963	268	1968	414	1973	222
1964	179	1969	237	1974	354
1965	329	1970	238	1975	392
1966	562	1971	286	1976	363
1967	491	1972	214	1977	539
				1978	482
				1979	441

Source: Institute of Chartered Financial Analysts, *1979-1980 Supplement to 1977-1978 Directory of Members.* Charlottesville, Va.: ICFA, 1979, p. 5.

because of its importance in this regard, it is printed at the end of this chapter (see below).

A careful review of this checklist of criteria indicates what security analysts want to know from and about corporations they analyze; it explicitly relates to portions of the Questionnaire sent to CFAs and investor relations specialists (Part II, Question 2, CFA; Part II, Question 3, IR specialists).

CHECKLIST OF CRITERIA FOR EVALUATING FINANCIAL COMMUNICATIONS EFFORT

Qualification Questions (Mandatory for each subcommittee's evaluation form)

1. To your knowledge, during the past year has the management of this company suppressed or misrepresented material facts adverse to the company and/or its operations or outlook?
2. In your opinion, are any accounting or other managerial practices of this company materially misleading?

(If you have answered either question in the affirmative, do not proceed with the rating of this company but contact the subcommittee chairman. An affirmative answer to either question by two or more subcommittee members will disqualify the company from being considered in this year's ratings.)

Note: The percentage weights appearing after each major category title (below) can be distributed to subcategories in whatever manner seems appropriate to each subcommittee.

I. *Annual Report* (40% to 50% of total weight)
    A. *Financial Highlights*– (Is it clear and unambigous?)
    B. *President's Letter Review*–(Does it hit the highlights of the year in an objective manner? Is it relevant to the company's results and candid in appraising problems?) It should include:
        1. Review of the year
        2. Insights into operating rates, unit production levels and selling prices
        3. Acquisitions and divestments, if any
        4. Government business, if material
        5. Capital expenditures program; start-up expenses
        6. Research and development efforts
        7. Employment costs, labor relations, union contracts
        8. Energy cost and availability
        9. Environmental and OSHA costs
        10. Backlogs
        11. New products
        12. Legislative and regulatory developments
        13. Outlook
    C. *Officers and Directors*
        1. Age, background, responsibilities of officers
        2. Description of company organization
        3. Outside affiliations of directors

    4.   Principal personnel changes

D. *Statement of Corporate Goals*

What are the short- and long-term corporate goals and how and when does management expect to achieve them? (This section could be included in several areas of the report but separate treatment is preferred.)

E. *Discussions of Divisional and/or Segment Operations*
1. How complete is the breakdown of sales, materials, costs, overhead, and earnings?
2. Are the segments logical for analytical purposes?
3. Are unusual developments explained with management's response included?
4. Note comparisons with relevant industry developments to include:
   a. Market size and growth
   b. Market penetration
   c. Geographical divergences
5. Foreign operations:
   a. Revenues, including export sales
   b. Consolidated foreign earnings vs. equity interests
   c. Market and/or regional trends
   d. Tax status

F. *Financial Summary and Footnotes*
1. Statement of accounting principles, including explanation of changes and their effects
2. Adjustments to EPS for dilution
3. Unconsolidated subsidiaries and affiliates—operating information
4. Sources and applications of funds
5. Tax accounting—investment tax credits; breakdown of current and deferred for U.S. and non-U.S. tax jurisdictions; reconciliation of effective and statutory tax rates
6. Clarity of explanation of currency exchange rate accounting
   a. Impact on earnings from Balance Sheet translation (FAS No. 8)
   b. Indication of "operating" or Income Account Effect of exchange rate fluctuations
7. Property accounts and Depreciation policies:
   a. Methods and asset lives used for tax and for financial reporting
   b. Quantification of effect on reported earnings of use of different method and/or asset lives for tax purposes
8. Investments: valuation
9. Inventories: method of valuation and identifying different methods for various product or geographic segments
10. Leases, rentals: terms and liability
11. Debt repayment schedules
12. Pension funds: costs charged to income; interest rate and wage inflation assumptions; amount of any unfunded past service liability; amortization period for unfunded liability
13. Capital expenditure programs and forecasts, including costs for environmental purposes
14. Acquisitions and divestitures (if material):
    a. Description of activity and operating results
    b. Type of financial transaction
    c. Effect on reported sales and earnings

        d.   Quantification of purchased acquisitions or small poolings that do not require restatement of prior years' results. (When restating for pooling, both old and new data are useful for comparison.)

  15.   Year-end adjustments

  16.   Restatement of quarterly reports to year-end accounting basis

  17.   Research and Development and new products: amount and types of outlays and forecasts

  18.   Contingent liabilities

  19.   Derivation of number of shares used for calculating primary and fully-diluted earnings per share

  20.   Treatment of other relevant matters (extraordinary charges, loss provisions, bad debt reserves, etc.)

  21.   Goodwill—amount being amortized and number of years

  22.   Ten-year Statistical Summary:
        a.   Adequacy of income account and balance sheet detail
        b.   Helpfulness of "non-statement" data (e.g. number of employees, adjusted number of shares, price of stock, capital expenditures, etc.)

II. *Quarterly Reports* (Together with III, below, 30% to 40% of total weight)
    A.   Depth of commentary on operating results and developments
    B.   Discussion of new products, management changes, problem areas
    C.   Degree of detail or profit and loss statement including divisional or segmental breakdown
    D.   Inclusion of a balance sheet
    E.   Restatement of all prior and current year quarters for major pooling acquisitions and quantification of effect of purchase acquisitions and/or disposals
    F.   Breakout of non-recurring or exceptional income or expense items including effects from inventory valuation and foreign exchange translation factors
    G.   Explicit statement of accounting principles underlying the quarterly statements
    H.   Timeliness of receiving reports

III. *Other Published Material* (See II, above).
    A.   Availability of proxy statements
    B.   Annual meeting report: available with questions and answers
    C.   Addresses to analysts' groups: available with questions and answers
    D.   Statistical supplements and fact books
    E.   Company magazines, newsletters, explanatory pamphlets
    F.   Press releases: Are they sent to shareholders and analysts?
    G.   How are documents filed with public agencies made available (SEC, Federal Trade Commission, Dept. of Labor, Court Cases, etc.)? Does the company disseminate all material information in 10-K, 10-Q, and similar reports?

IV. *Personal Contacts* (20% to 30% of total weight)
    A.   Is there a designated and advertised individual(s) for shareholder and analyst contacts?
    B.   Interviews:
       1.   Knowledgeability and responsiveness of company contact
       2.   Access to policymakers and operational people
       3.   Candor in discussing negative developments
    C.   Presentations to analyst groups: frequency and content
    D.   Company-sponsored field trips and meetings
    E.   Annual meetings:
       1.   Accessibility
       2.   Worthwhile to shareholders and analysts?

3

Trends in Corporate-Supplied Information

INTRODUCTION

Corporate and financial information, presented in an understandable form, is a major determinant of investment value in the capital market. Generally, the data are the basis upon which informed decision-making by investors takes place. Moreover, on much of this information, the SEC sets standards of "materiality" which publicly traded corporations must meet in their disclosure of information. This requirement of materiality may affect investors' decisions concerning the value of securities. SEC requirements are reinforced by the practices and rules of the accounting profession, which they dominate: the AICPA, the Accounting Principles Board (APB), and more recently, the Financial Accounting Standards Board, which has succeeded the Accounting Principles Board.

On an annual basis, at least through the annual report, corporations are required to disclose financial information audited by public accounting firms. The corporation must present balance sheets, income statements, changes in financial position, and statements of capital surplus and retained earnings, together with suitable footnotes. The auditing firm, in preparing these documents, must affirm that the corporation has followed "generally accepted accounting principles applied on a consistent basis" (GAAP). The rules of financial disclosure are set forth in the APBs and the FASBs listed in Tables 17 and 18.

In recent years, the SEC's attitude toward financial disclosure has begun to change. Whereas historically the emphasis was on the disclosure of historical cost, past-oriented information, the SEC is moving now toward the supplementary adoption of rules relating to future-oriented information. This is the distinction between "hard" (historical) and "soft" (forecasted) financial information. The objective of financial reporting is shifting from the stewardship concept (protection of assets) to the information concept (investors' decision-making approach). As Beaver reports:

> Recently, former FASB Chairman Marshall Armstrong commented on substantial opposition to adopting an information perspective with respect to the role of

Table 17.   Accounting Principles Board Opinions

1.	New Depreciation Guidelines and Rules	Nov 1962
2.	Accounting for "Investment Credit"	Dec 1962
3.	The Statement for Source and Application of Funds	Oct 1963
4.	Accounting for "Investment Credit" (Amending APB No. 2)	Mar 1964
5.	Reporting of Leases in Financial Statements of Lessee	Sep 1964
6.	Status of Accounting Research Bulletins	Oct 1965
7.	Accounting for Leases in Financial Statements of Lessors	May 1966
8.	Accounting for the Cost of Pension Plans	Nov 1966
9.	Reporting the Results of Operation	Dec 1966
10.	Omnibus Opinions–1966	Dec 1966
11.	Accounting for Income Taxes	Dec 1967
12.	Omnibus Opinions–1967	Dec 1967
13.	Amending Paragraph 6 of APB No. 9, Application to Commercial Banks	Mar 1969
14.	Accounting for Convertible Debt and Debt Issues With Stock Purchase Warrants	Mar 1969
15.	Earnings Per Share	May 1969
16.	Business Combination	Aug 1970
17.	Intangible Assets	Aug 1970
18.	The Equity Method of Accounting for Investments in Common Stock	Mar 1971
19.	Reporting Changes in Financial Position	Mar 1971
20.	Accounting Changes	Jul 1971
21.	Interest on Receivables and Payables	Aug 1971
22.	Disclosure of Accounting Policies	Apr 1972
23.	Accounting for Income Taxes–Special Areas	Apr 1972
24.	Accounting for Income Taxes–Investments in Common Stocks Accounted for by the Equity Method	Apr 1972
25.	Accounting for Stock Issued to Employees	Oct 1972
26.	Early Extinguishment of Debt	Oct 1972
27.	Accounting for Lease Transactions by Manufacturers or Dealer Lessors	Nov 1972
28.	Interim Financial Reporting	May 1973
29.	Accounting for Non-Monetary Transactions	May 1973
30.	Reporting the Results of Operations–Reporting the Effects of Disposal of a Segment of a Business, and Extraordinary, Unusual and Infrequently Occurring Events and Transactions	Jun 1973
31.	Disclosure of Lease Commitments by Lessees	Jun 1973

Table 18.   Financial Accounting Standard Board Opinions

1.	Disclosure of Foreign Currency Translation Information	Dec 1973
2.	Accounting for Research and Development Cost	Oct 1974
3.	Reporting Accounting Changes in Interim Financial Statements	Dec 1974
4.	Reporting Gains and Losses from Extinguishment of Debt	Mar 1975
5.	Accounting for Contingencies	Mar 1975
6.	Classification of Short-Term Obligations Expected to be Refinanced	May 1975
7.	Accounting and Reporting by Development Stage Enterprises	Jun 1975
8.	Accounting for the Translation of Foreign Currency Transactions and Foreign Currency Financial Statements	Oct 1975
9.	Accounting for Income Taxes—Oil and Gas Producing Companies	Oct 1975
10.	Extension of "Grandfather" Provisions for Business Combinations	Oct 1975
11.	Accounting for Contingencies—Transaction Method	Dec 1975
12.	Accounting for Certain Marketable Securities	Dec 1975
13.	Accounting for Leases	Nov 1976
14.	Financial Reporting for Segment of a Business Enterprise	Dec 1976
15.	Accounting by Debtors and Creditors for Troubled Debt Restructurings	Jun 1977
16.	Prior Period Adjustments	Jun 1977

financial statements. According to Armstrong, this is viewed as a shift away from the traditional perspective of stewardship and from a historical cost, past-events orientation to financial reporting. However, one of the most important aspects of the FASB's statement of objectives is the reformulation of the stewardship concept so that it becomes subsumed under the user, decision-making approach. It is contended that stewardship should not be viewed in a narrow custodianship context but in a broader, performance evaluation role. According to this view, management's responsibility is more than merely safekeeping assets, but also includes the responsibility of earning a return on those assets.[1]

In the present research, Part III of the questionnaire sent to the NIRI and CFAs was designed to compare quantitatively the attitudes between the two groups on matters of selected "hard" and "soft" information and other related matters. Part III of the questionnaire surveyed opinions, in regard to investment decision-making, as follows:

1.   "Hard" information—Questions 1-6
2.   "Soft" information—Questions 7-13
3.   Information "overload"—Questions 14-15

"HARD" INFORMATION

Among the latest in a long series of disclosure requirements are business segment reporting (FASB 14) and the capitalization of leases on the balance sheet (FASB 13). Business segment reporting (Part III-Question 1), which requires corporations to disclose sales and pre-tax earnings by major product or divisional activity was initially and strongly opposed by corporations. Security analysts, however, have always been eager to obtain this information, so they welcomed this action by the SEC. This information greatly facilitates the security analyst's work, permitting him to evaluate the source and quality of earnings from different corporate activities. It is especially useful in the appraisal of conglomerates and multinational companies. Still, the security analysts desire even more detailed breakdowns. Corporations complained about disclosing this information, since it presumably allowed their competitors to gain more information about their market share and penetration.

Capitalizing leases (Part III-Question 2) is another potentially controversial issue. Corporations historically have done a great deal of "off balance sheet" financing, which was not officially incorporated on the balance sheet. This has allowed them to preserve debt ratios within appropriate limits, while doing a substantial amount of debt financing not otherwise shown on the balance sheet. Capitalized leases can alter the ratios substantially and presumably affect investor perceptions about the riskiness of securities.

A common complaint of investors is that the footnotes to the financial statements are written in an obscure language that only CPAs can understand.

This is a legitimate complaint, since there are 25 million direct investors in the United States, most of whom are not professionally trained to understand financial statements and the associated footnotes. It has been suggested that footnotes be written in "plain English" (Part III-Question 3) as an aid to the small investor. If pressure eventually builds for this change, this doubtless will become an SEC requirement.

In recent years, the SEC has suggested auditor review of corporate interim financial statements (Part III-Question 4); for example, quarterly financial reports. As H. Zane Robbins notes, SEC "suggestions" become tantamount to orders. He says:

> Perhaps the first thing to be said about the new Securities and Exchange Commission's "requirements" for interim reports to shareholders is that they aren't requirements at all. They're "suggestions."[2]

Corporations generally have resisted this development, but it is likely welcomed by auditors, who increase their fees, and by security analysts, who gain in the quality of interim reporting. Officially, the interim statements remain unaudited, but unofficially they become at least quasi-audited.

Explicit disclosure of auditors' fees (Part III-Question 5) in the annual report or 10-K is not required by the SEC. Although these fees can run to substantial amounts, the auditors say they usually are not material. Some investors, however, might be surprised at the magnitude of these fees and question the cost-benefits of this accounting activity. While shareholders have the right to know and gain this information at the company's annual shareholders' meeting, it is not otherwise easily obtained. For some reason, shareholders seldom seek this information, thus suggesting that it is unimportant to their informational needs.

Similarly, explicit disclosure of investor relations costs (Part III-Question 6) is virtually never made, yet the increasing use of investor relations activities by corporations during the past 10 years must mean a rapid growth of investor relations costs to be assumed by the corporate sector. Without information on this matter, investors and security analysts can hardly appraise the cost-benefits of investor relations activities. One possible implication of the efficient markets hypothesis (see Chapter 4) is that corporations, since they cannot really affect the value of their securities through investor relations, probably waste a great deal of money on redundant investor relations efforts. Corporations spend substantial sums on their investor relations activities, yet shareholders seem to demonstrate little or no interest in this subject.

One observation is in order concerning "hard" information. Over the years, as new APBs and FASBs were promulgated, corporations and their investor relations specialists have generally opposed the additional disclosure requirements. Corporations believe that it is an encroachment on managerial prerogatives and free enterprise, which results in added costs with no corresponding benefits. Security analysts, on the other hand, have generally favored this disclosure trend, because it produces more useful information not otherwise conveniently available, and because the costs of this disclosure are borne, not by the security analysts, but by the corporations and, by implication, its shareholders. Or, as Beaver observes:

> . . . analysts typically have been active advocates of the "need" for additional disclosure of various sorts. This is hardly surprising. The analyst community is an industry whose product is information, analysis and interpretation. One major factor of production to this industry is disclosures by corporations. However, the costs of disclosures are borne in large part by the companies' shareholders (and perhaps indirectly by customers and employees), rather than by the analysts themselves. The analysts undoubtedly incur some cost in obtaining and processing the disclosures, but it is only a portion of the total cost of disclosure. Hence, corporate disclosures constitute a factor of production that will not be fully paid by the industry using that factor, and this constitutes a form of subsidy. Asking the analyst community about the potential desirability of increased disclosure may be tantamount to asking an industry if it wants a subsidy. We should not be too surprised when that industry responds in the affirmative.[3]

"SOFT" INFORMATION

"Soft" information refers to corporate management's intentions and forecasts. The questions are whether these should be disclosed and whether the information is useful in the investment decision-making process. A priori, corporations would be expected to say "no," and security analysts would be expected to say a qualified "yes."

The major corporate reason is that it leaves the management, board of directors, and the auditing firms open to major legal liabilities, because it relates to information that contains a high uncertainty element (the future). This information, if disclosed, would be used by investors in making investment decisions. Management, therefore, is afraid of major shareholder lawsuits when the forecasts go astray.

Security analysts approve of future-oriented information, but they also see it as a potential invasion of their own professional standing, since as part of their regular work they make forecasts of corporate sales, earnings, and security values in their recommendations to investors and portfolio managers. "Soft" information, therefore, implies a substitution of corporate forecasts for analysts' forecasts, which would presumably reduce the importance of a security analyst to his own organization and to the capital market.

"Soft" information, except in a highly limited way, has not been mandated by the SEC, but some observers think such action is not too many years away. At least the SEC has changed its posture to encourage corporations to disclose current value and future-oriented information. Beaver notes:

> Certainly the SEC has actively altered its long-standing discouragement and prohibition of current value and future-oriented data in SEC filings. ASR No. 190 on replacement costs and the releases on management forecasts (Release nos. 33-5581 and 33-5699) are two recent illustrations. Moreover, in an amicus curiae brief filed in the Gerstle v. Gamble-Skogmo litigation, the SEC took the position that failure to disclose such information may, in certain circumstances, constitute a violation of the securities acts. This trend is being reinforced by recommendations of the analysts' community for more disclosure of future-oriented and interpretive data.[4]

In the Questionnaire, replacement cost information (Part III-Question 7) refers to the SEC requirement that firms with inventories and fixed assets of over $100 million must restate these on a replacement cost basis (current value) in a footnote to the financial statements. Many companies note the difficulty of their estimating these current values, asserting that this kind of information is meaningless to investors. The apparent SEC purpose in this disclosure is to account for the accumulated impact of past inflation on the replacement of productive capacity, which is otherwise stated on the balanced sheet at book value (i.e., at historical cost). This information is future-oriented in that it estimates the cost of replacement if this should take place in a very short period of time. Currently, security analysts appear to make little use of these estimates in determining investment values.

Loosely connected to replacement costs is management's expected capital spending (Part III-Question 9) during the next year. Investors and security analysts rely on this information for clues to management's expectations of future growth and the general economic outlook.

Dividend policy (Part III-Question 8), stated in terms of a payout ratio (point estimate or range), is not uncommon among corporations; however, neither is it routinely disclosed by a majority of public corporations. If one can estimate earnings, given dividend policy, future dividends are easily estimated. This is surely one of the strong suits of security analysts, and a matter upon which they often rest their reputations. Future dividends are an obvious matter of importance to investors, since in certain valuation models (e.g., the Gordon model) dividends are what investors capitalize in the stock market.

Like a target payout (dividend) ratio, investors and security analysts also appear to prefer a target debt-equity ratio of a corporation (Part III-Question 10). Knowledge of this ratio, projected into the future, can be valuable in the assessment of management's attitude toward the corporation's debt limits, financial risk class, and potential need for future equity offerings.

The center of the controversy regarding "soft" information is the question of management's forecasting of sales, earnings, and earnings per share (Part III-Questions 11, 12, and 13), and disclosing these estimates in an appropriate format with an enumeration of underlying assumptions.

William S. Gray, Chairman of the FAF Special Committee on Corporate Forecasts, listed the elements of a continuous forecasting system that should be adopted by corporations desiring to disclose their forecasts:

1.   Forecasting should be voluntary, not mandatory, at this time.
2.   Once public forecasting has begun, forecast statements should be disclosed on a continuing basis.
3.   Forecasts should be broadly disseminated on a regular basis.
4.   The forecast period, for the present, should be the current and next fiscal year.
5.   The forecast should be specific for sales, pre-tax earnings, net earnings, and earnings per share.
6.   Forecasts should be qualified by some expression of their tentative character.
7.   Statement of assumptions on which the forecast is based.[5]

Gray favors corporate forecasting, if done properly; he concludes that ". . . the individual investor may have greater confidence in the market mechanism as a result of receiving directly important corporate information. . . ." In a similar call for corporate disclosure of financial forecasting, George S. Bissell states:

> I regard financial forecasting as an extension of the broader responsibility of corporate disclosure. Furthermore, it is a widely accepted assumption that buyers and sellers of securities today depend to a substantial degree on future expectation as a major aspect of the investment decision-making process. The conclusion seems inescapable that the more broadly reliable information that is disseminated throughout the investment community, the greater will be the tendency of security prices to remain at or near "true investment value," contributing to a more stable price pattern. Hence the issue today is not *whether* but *how* to undertake appropriate financial forecasting, and I would add, *to whom* and *by what* means.[6]

Other authors also strongly recommend the utility of forecasting and its disclosure by corporations, as stated below:

> . . . the negative stance of management toward publishing earnings forecasts is difficult to justify given available approaches to publication without disclosure of internal strategies. Considering the position of the SEC and the Sommer's Committee, can management afford the posture it has taken? Should not one prepare himself for moving in the direction of what appears to be an extension of the reporting process?[7]

On the other side of the issue are equally strong opponents of management forecasts. Harvey Kapnick, Chairman of the Board of Arthur Andersen, vigorously resists the disclosure of corporate forecasts. He states the reasons for this adversary position:

> The problems related to the publication, by management, of financial forecasts revolve around the two principal propositions I have stated: first, forecasting is a function of the investor and not of management; and second, since a forecast is just that—a prediction about an uncertain future—the forecast is likely to be misleading if prepared by someone other than the user.[8]

After surveying 600 CFAs, Russell Fuller and Richard Metcalf see corporate forecast disclosure as useful to investors but not to security analysts. (This conclusion will be further examined in Chapter 5.) From the survey results, they surmise that:

> It appears to us that the controversy surrounding the disclosure of management forecasts is another example of outsiders, albeit with good intentions, hindering the investment process while trying to improve it. Logic and our survey would suggest that management forecasts are useful information for the investing public, but superfluous data for security analysts, who feel they can obtain the information without any formal disclosure policy.

> Financial analysts apparently also feel there is a tradeoff between the cost of disclosure and the value of the additional information. Many of the CFA's surveyed commented that the effort and cost of complying with the SEC's original proposal for disclosing management's forecasts wouldn't be offset by the additional information provided. And clearly, financial analysts do NOT feel they need whatever benefits would be provided, if any, from having the forecasts of management audited. It is to be hoped that the SEC, management and the accounting professions can work together to improve the quality of *current* disclosures before exploring their other new avenues that may dissipate the energies of those involved while offering little, if any, reward to the public.[9]

Since the SEC, in 1972, announced its interest in compulsory disclosure of corporate forecasts (which is still an interest of the Commission), a sizeable literature has grown up on the comparative merits of management forecasting and its disclosure. As it currently stands, the issue is far from settled by the SEC, the accounting profession, public corporations and their investor relations staffs, security analysts, and the investing public generally.

INFORMATION OVERLOAD

Corporations believe that more disclosure is being required by the SEC than is necessary to ensure efficient capital markets (Part III-Question 14). Corporations and their shareholders bear the costs of this additional information output. Modern academicians would probably agree and might suggest that information, like any product, be assessed by a cost-benefit analysis. In this connection, Beaver states the academic position:

> The regulation of disclosure is essentially an economic issue, amenable to an analysis of the various consequences of disclosure. Instead, a legalistic approach pervades much of the current approach to disclosure. As a result, there is a danger that the promulgation of disclosure rules will inflict more damage on investors, the intended beneficiaries of the securities acts, than if there were no regulation at all.

> The current viewpoint is epitomized by the concept of information "needs." According to this notion, it is virtually impossible for the investor to rationally function without certain information necessary to the investment decision. Similarly, it has been argued that investors have "inherent rights" with respect to corporate disclosures. The effect of this approach is to insulate disclosure policies from an analysis of their economic consequences.[10]

Concerning the cost-benefit tradeoff, Arthur B. Laffer sees "information overkill":

> Additional requirements for the production and dissemination of information appear at best to be redundant. At worst, of course, additional requirements will add to the already burdensome administrative and compliance costs. This additional burden will tend to make everyone worse off, with no compensating improvement anywhere.[11]

Standing on the other side of the question, security analysts, accountants, and securities attorneys likely prefer the additional information, especially as these costs are borne, not by them, but by the corporation. Security analysts appear to have an insatiable appetite for corporate information; "more" rather than "less" is their byword, since they constitute an "information processing industry" of major size.

Finally, to evaluate further the idea of "information overload," the investor relations specialists and security analysts were both asked to list any information ("hard" or "soft") that should be disclosed by corporations to help investors in their decision-making (Question No. 15). One would expect security analysts to be more responsive than investor relations specialists to this question. See Chapter 5 for detailed results, and Chapter 6 for summarized results.

4

Modern Investment Theory

INTRODUCTION

Modern investment theory (MIT) may be viewed as the formalization and convergence of two important streams of development in financial theory—the efficient markets hypothesis and the mean-variance portfolio theory—which, when combined, produce the capital asset pricing model. Modern investment theory has been on the academic scene for only the past 15 or 20 years, but today academic journals of finance are dominated by these ideas. Modern investment theory is a highly rigorous, quantitative discipline in both theory and empirical testing; it combines elements of microeconomic theory, statistics, mathematics, econometrics, and modern financial models and concepts.

In the academic world, modern investment theory has largely replaced the traditional roles and positions of technical analysis (the Dow Theory), fundamental analysis (Graham and Dodd), and older portfolio prescriptions of "beating the market." The language of modern investment theory is entirely different, using such terms as "random walks," "alphas" and "betas," "systematic risk" and "unsystematic risk," "variance" and "covariance," "efficient frontiers," the "capital asset pricing model," and so on. None of these terms is to be found in traditional textbooks on investments.

The efficient markets hypothesis, once considered bizarre in the investment literature, is now generally (although not universally) accepted by academicians. This hypothesis states that securities prices "instantaneously" reflect all knowable and relevant information that flows into the capital market. Securities prices and capital markets are considered "efficient" in the sense that: (a) security prices react rapidly to new information, and (b) investors will be unable to earn above-average rates of return on securities. The requirements for sustaining an efficient market assume certain economic postulates: (a) fully competitive markets; (b) rational investors; (c) widespread availability of low-cost information; and (d) continuous low-cost trading. American capital markets appear, in general, to support these postulates, and much empirical testing by academicians has vindicated the efficient markets hypothesis. Academicians consider this hypothesis to be an idealized representation of capital markets. It may not be literally true, but it is sufficiently true to give useful and testable insights into the behavior of securities prices and capital markets.

The efficient markets hypothesis is cast into three testable forms, depending on the level of information or knowledge about securities being considered. The first, and the oldest, is the "weak form test," or the random walk hypothesis, which focuses on the statistical behavior of stock price changes over time. In this respect, it is a direct challenge to technical analysis. The "semi-strong form test" focuses on how rapidly prices adjust to publicly known information, such as corporate annual reports, quarterly reports, press releases, etc.; it is a direct challenge to security analysts. The "strong form test" goes a step further and focuses on all information that is known or knowable about a company; it is a direct challenge to large institutional investors and their analysts. For each of these three tests, the evidence is strongest for the "weak form" and is less voluminous and more uncertain in the "strong form" tests.

Each of these tests will be summarized briefly in terms of its development, methodology, findings, and implications for investment practitioners; then modern portfolio theory and the capital asset pricing model will be discussed.

RANDOM WALK HYPOTHESIS AND TECHNICIANS

The random walk hypothesis, or "weak form test," dates back to 1900 when Louis Bachelier[1] found that commodity prices and government bonds follow a "random walk" (an unpredictable path). Other early works on the random character of stock price changes occurred during the 1930s (Working,[2] Cowles and Jones[3]), but this important idea remained largely neglected until the 1950s, when Maurice G. Kendall[4] and M.F.M. Osborne[5] published research on the subject. Kendall discovered that serial correlation in weekly changes of stock market prices did not exist. This meant that past stock prices cannot be used to predict future stock prices, contrary to the position held by technical analysts. He noted that "such serial correlation as is present in these series is so weak as to dispose at once of any possibility of being able to use them for prediction."[6] Osborne, likewise, in testing daily stock price changes, discovered random behavior akin to "Brownian motion" in physics.[7]

After these early states, a voluminous amount of literature was published on the testing of random behavior of stock price changes. Some important authors in the field are: Granger and Morgenstern;[8] Fama;[9], [10] Roberts;[11] Cheng and Deets;[12] Shiskin;[13] Alexander;[14] Cootner;[15] Levy;[16] Jensen and Bennington;[17] Jen;[18] Kruizenga;[19] and Boness.[20] Most evidence supported the random walk hypothesis, although a few noteworthy studies produced contrary findings; e.g., Robert A. Levy.[21]

Throughout the history of testing the random walk hypothesis, two general types of empirical tests have been made: (1) the analysis of stock price patterns, to see if cycles or trends persist, and (2) tests of technical trading rules, which are designed to simulate the work of technical analysts. Against these tests, two general benchmarks are used to determine the adequacy of the random walk models. One is the pure random walk, where statistical independence is obtained in the price series, so that, like a fair game, the expected mathematical outcome is zero. The second is a martingale process which allows for drift (trend) in the time series, but knowledge of the drift embodied in a mechanical trading rule (e.g., the use of statistical filters) cannot outperform a naive buy-hold strategy. That is, trading (filters) based on technical analysis is no more profitable than one's randomly selecting a group of stocks in the same risk class and simply holding them for the time horizon postulated.

For specific studies, Eugene F. Fama's work is especially important, since his name is the most often linked with the theory developed on "random walks" and "efficient markets."[22] In one study, using parametric statistics, Fama investigated the statistical property of independence in successive price changes for the 30 stocks contained in the Dow Jones Industrial Averages (DJIA) for the five-year period ending in 1962. He examined the daily changes in each of the stocks to determine, with lags up to 10 days, if any statistical dependency existed in these price series. If dependency existed, then serial correlations would be evident in the series—that is, there would be a linear relation of one price change (ΔP_t) to a subsequent price change ($\Delta P_t + 1$). The serial correlation coefficient between successive events in the same time series would indicate the value of the linear relation. Thus, correlation coefficient values of +1 or -1 would indicate a straight line, and support a conclusion of strong serial correlations (dependency); whereas a value of 0 or nearly 0 would indicate no serial correlation of practical significance. From these tests, Fama concluded that any statistical dependency (serial correlation) in the time series was too weak to be useful to the investor, and thus indicated that stock price movements follow a random walk.

In a second test, using nonparametric statistics, Fama[23] conducted a "runs" test of the directional signs (+, -, 0) of successive price changes on the 30 DJIA companies. If the "runs" tend to persist, they will give a value different from the number of runs expected from a perfectly random distribution. Fama found that, while one-day runs have a slight tendency to depart from randomness, when the tests are extended to 4, 9, and 16 days, the actual results conform exactly with a random distribution.

It is not surprising, therefore, that Fama saw the validation of the random walk hypothesis as a direct challenge to technical analysis.

> For the chartist, the challenge is straight-forward. If the random walk is a valid description of reality, the work of the chartist, like that of the astrologer, is of no real value in stock market analysis. The empirical evidence to date provides strong support for the random walk model.[24]

This challenge is specifically reflected in the Questionnaire in Statement 1 and 2 of Part IV.

The chartist or technician is a security analyst who predominantly practices technical analysis. He tends to be more interested in making "timing" decisions (when to buy) than "value" decisions (what to buy). He believes that history repeats itself in decipherable cycles, so that past patterns in stock price movements can be used as predictors of future price movements. Cycles tend to repeat themselves. In statistical terms, this means that the time series of stock price movements contain significant serial correlations. In practical terms, this means that he can earn above-average profits by playing these cycles or trends.

Technical analysts practice their "discipline" by a wide variety of techniques. These include Dow Theory, trend analysis, point and figure charts, support versus resistance levels, market breadth, and odd-lot transactions. Also, various economic phenomena are used as cyclical timing devices: money supply changes, interest rates, business cycles, and lead indicators. The idea is to "beat the crowd," using whatever clues or predictors are available from the stock market and/or economic time series themselves.

It is noteworthy that the tradition of fundamental security analysis (in the mainstream of Graham and Dodd) is almost as opposed to technical analysis as is the random walk position. Graham and Dodd state, "Forecasting security prices is not properly a part of security analysis."[25] They devote sections of their Chapter 53 to the following headings: 1. Chart Reading Not a Science; 2. Its Practice Cannot Be Continuously Successful; and 3. Theoretical Basis Open to Question.

Despite the opposition to technical analysis, the efficient markets hypothesis is also as opposed to fundamental analysis as the semi-strong and strong form tests of the efficient markets hypothesis suggest.

EFFICIENT MARKETS HYPOTHESIS AND SECURITY ANALYSTS

The semi-strong form of the efficient markets hypothesis is a much stronger test than the weak form, since it requires a greater level of knowledge and market efficiency. The semi-strong form asserts that all publicly known information about a corporation—or any subset of that information, such as earnings changes, dividend changes, or other fundamental factors—is fully embodied in, or already discounted by, its stock price. Furthermore, it asserts that information disclosed by a corporation is "instantaneously" (quickly) reflected in its stock price and in many instances is correctly anticipated by the stock price even before the disclosure is made. Therefore, further analysis of public data is fruitless and cannot lead, except by luck, to superior investment performance. Prices adjust to new information too rapidly for investors to take advantage of this movement.

In principle, it is clear that this position is a direct challenge to fundamental security analysts whose job is to examine company, industry, and macroeconomic data to determine which investment values will produce superior investment results. James H. Lorie and Mary T. Hamilton state:

> This stronger assertion has proved to be especially unacceptable and unpalatable to the financial community, since it suggests the fruitlessness of efforts to earn superior rates of return by the analysis of all public information. Although some members of the financial community were willing to accept the implications of the weaker assertion about the randomness of price changes and thereby to give up technical analysis, almost no members of the community were too willing to accept the implications of the stronger form and thereby to give up fundamental analysis.[26]

There are numerous studies that test the semi-strong form, almost all within the past 10 years. One important study concerned stock splits; it was based on the Wall Street adage that "a stock split increases the total value of the share outstanding because investors are more inclined to purchase lower price shares."[27] This study,[28] conducted by Fama, Fisher, Jensen, and Roll, examines security returns around split dates to see if there is any unusual behavior, and if so, to what extent it can be accounted for by relations between splits and other nonfundamental variables.[29] The test analyzed the speed and accuracy of the market's reaction to announced stock splits to see if such splits contain "new" information or if they have already been discounted by the market.

This test examined 940 splits (25 per cent or greater) of NYSE stocks during the period 1927-59. The test methodology focused on periods 30 months before and 30 months after each stock split announcement. Each stock was adjusted for its known movement against the stock market so that the residual value of the split, itself, could be isolated and examined. For example, if one stock over the long run goes up or down 10 per cent more than the market does, then this movement was "adjusted out," thus isolating the performance of the stock price in relation to the split announcement only. This enables one to test whether the post-split price performance of the stock is greater than would be expected from the split itself.

This study concluded that the market is efficient in anticipating stock splits and that nearly all of the "information content" of a stock split has been fully discounted before the announcement. Even when cash dividend increases are frequently associated with stock splits, the market is generally efficient in anticipating this development. Or, as Fama said:

> . . . although the behavior of post-split returns will be very different depending on whether or not dividend "increases" occur, and in spite of the fact that a large majority of split securities do experience dividend "increases," when all splits are examined together, subsequent to the split there is not net movement up or

down in the cumulative average residuals. Thus, apparently the market makes unbiased forecasts of the implications of a split for future dividends, and these forecasts are fully reflected in the prices of the security by the end of the split month. After considerably more data analysis than can be summarized, FFJR conclude that their results lend considerable support to the conclusion that the stock market is efficient, at least with respect to its ability to adjust to the information implicit in a split.[30]

The subject of stock splits is germane to this study (Part IV-Question 5) because corporations and their investor relations specialists appear to believe that stock splits are good, especially when associated with cash dividend increases. They tend to think stock prices will rise after the split announcement is made. It is unlikely, however, that security analysts accept this idea, since it is their job to anticipate and correctly price the information content of stock splits.

In another important study testing the semi-strong form, Ray Ball and Philip Brown examined the market's capacity to anticipate annual earnings per share of corporations before publication of annual reports. Using the Standard and Poor's Compustat tapes on 261 large corporations and adjusting for the general trend of the market, they found that "most of the information contained in reported annual earnings is anticipated by the market before the annual report is released."[31] This finding is not surprising, since most of this information has been disclosed previously by corporations in their interim reports and press releases. Most corporations and security analysts believe that the annual report is the most important document published by a corporation, but, according to the efficient markets hypothesis, the annual report does not provide any really new information to investors.

Another question discussed in this study is whether good news is disseminated by corporations to the market more promptly than bad news (Part IV-Question 6). Victor Neiderhoffer and Patrick S. Regan investigated this question by examining the news-reporting behavior of two sets of 50 NYSE companies, each regarding earnings releases: (1) those having the sharpest increases for the year, and (2) those having the sharpest declines for the year. They concluded that 88 per cent of those in Group 1 released their earnings right away (within two months of the end of the fiscal year), while only 40 per cent of those in Group 2 released their earnings within this time period.[32]

This news-reporting lag raises some question about the efficiency of the market in the discounting of bad news and is a valuable area for further research. It also raises the question of the differential attitudes of investor relations specialists and security analysts toward the efficiency of investor relations programs in promptly disseminating all material information necessary for intelligent investment decision-making (Part IV-Question 6).

Various other tests have been conducted on the semi-strong form; most of them validate the efficacy of the efficient markets model. These tests generally uphold the view that markets are efficient and quickly respond to news, and that published reports of security analysts contribute little to investment decision-making because the information presented has already been assimilated by the market. "The most general implication of the efficient markets hypothesis is that most security analysis is logically incomplete and valueless."[33] This means that the economic value of security analysis is low.

Henry C. Wallich reasons that there are probably too many security analysts, and that a substantially fewer number would be necessary to assure the efficiency of the market.

> It is important for the good functioning of the economy that securities be correctly priced. Incorrect pricing can produce serious disturbance. Here is the main social contribution of securities analysis. But approximately correct pricing could probably be obtained with a fraction of the manpower now employed in securities analysis.[34]

With their jobs in jeopardy, security analysts logically would strongly oppose the "low economic value" asserted by proponents of the efficient markets hypothesis (Part IV-Question 8). Since corporations spend a great deal of time and money on cultivating a following by security analysts, they probably would concur in the importance of security analysis. They might even encourage the population of security analysts to grow, not to contract, so as to have even lager and more sophisticated audiences with whom to communicate. This might be the case if most investor relations specialists believe their companies' stock are undervalued (Questionnaire, Investor Relations, Part I-Question 7).

STRONG FORM TESTS AND INSTITUTIONAL INVESTORS

The strong form of the efficient markets hypothesis holds that even sophisticated investment research by the largest investors (institutional investors with specialized security analysts: pension funds, banks, mutual funds, larger portfolio managers) cannot lead to superior investment results. The reason is the same as in the semi-strong form, which asserts that all known and knowable information about corporations is already discounted in market prices. Indeed, the strong form claims that even insiders (under the SEC rule called 10-B-5), and specialists on the NYSE cannot earn abnormal returns in the market by the benefit of their superior knowledge.

The evidence in support of the strong form is scanty compared with tests of the other forms of the efficient markets hypothesis. Evidence in support of the strong form is discernible in studies by Diefenback,[35] and to a lesser extent in Friend, Blume and Crockett.[36] Other studies, such as those by Miller,[37] Wallich,[38] and Kuehner,[39] challenge the efficient markets thesis. Several of these studies employ the capital asset pricing model (discussed in a later section).

One may conclude at this point that the strong form is far from being validated and that further research is needed. Still, there are an increasing number of believers in the efficient markets hypothesis, even the strong form; larger institutional investors are manifesting this belief in a growing volume of investable funds being placed in Index Funds, which are discussed in a later section.

MODERN PORTFOLIO THEORY

Modern portfolio theory and the capital asset pricing model represent an important advance in finance theory. No longer does one look at securities one at a time, as in conventional security analysis, but at securities in collectives, i.e., in portfolios. This alters the way the risk-return characteristics of securities are viewed and priced. A number of academicians have suggested that the only appropriate way to manage large common stock portfolios is to use Index Funds. Paradoxically, this means "managing" an unmanaged fund. An understanding of this development begins with Markowitz.

Markowitz Portfolio Theory

Harry Markowitz's famous monograph *Portfolio Selection* was published in 1959. This book presented a new framework for investment decision-making under uncertainty and introduced concepts of expected returns, variances and co-variances for ones achieving optimal portfolios. As Markowitz said, "A good portfolio is more than a long list of stocks and bonds. It is a balanced whole. . . ."[40]

Working from the principle that investors like returns and dislike risk, Markowitz showed that optimal diversification is a function of the degree of correlation among security returns.

> If correlation among security returns were "perfect"—if returns on all securities moved up and down together in perfect unison—diversification could do nothing to eliminate risk. The fact that security returns are highly correlated, but not perfectly correlated, implies that diversification can reduce risk but not eliminate it.[41]

To gain the best portfolio, investors can select securities which give the highest return for a given level of risk, or securities which minimize risk for a given level of return. Portfolios meeting these conditions are defined as efficient; i.e., they fall on the efficient frontier. Otherwise, they are considered inefficient, which means that other portfolios available for selection are superior to the inefficient ones.

Mathematically, the portfolio problem can be stated in two equations where E denotes expected return and V denotes variance or risk as a function of the variance of each individual stock and the co-variance of each stock with every other stock in the portfolio. Symbolically,

$$E = \sum_{i}^{N} X_i R_i \qquad \text{(Equation 1)}$$

where:

E = expected return on a portfolio

X_i = proportion of total fund invested in security i

R_i = rate of return on security i

N = number of securities in the portfolio

and the variance of the portfolio is stated as:

$$V = \sum_{i}^{N} \sum_{j}^{N} \sigma_{ij} X_i X_j \qquad \text{(Equation 2)}$$

where:

σ_{ij} = the covariance between Ri and Rj

X_i = proportion of fund invested in security i

X_j = proportion of fund invested in security j

This formulation gives the E (return) and V (risk) of each portfolio analyzed. First, it shows why diversification works. A portfolio of stocks can nearly always be selected which achieves the same return as one stock (a one-stock portfolio), but since stocks are not perfectly correlated, the risk of a portfolio is less than the risk of owning one stock. According to this view, it is rational to diversify; it is irrational not to diversify. Second, the formulation shows that some diversified portfolios are better than others. For example, two portfolios may have the same E's (returns), but different V's (risks). The lowest V is always preferable in this case, assuming investors are risk averse (they want the lowest risk possible, given some level of returns). Consequently, when all portfolios are analyzed in terms of their E-V parameters, some will be found to be efficient and the rest to be inefficient.

Graphically, portfolios examined can be arranged as follows: when E is returns on the vertical axis, and V is risk on the horizontal axis, then:

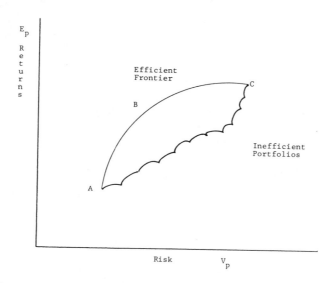

Portfolios lying on the curve ABC are "efficient," because they present the highest returns for the risks assumed. Curve ABC is thus the "efficient frontier." All portfolios below the curve are "inefficient," since the investor can always move to a superior E-V position, and optimally, to some desired point on the curve ABC.

Sharpe's Index Model

Because of computational complexities involved in large portfolios, William F. Sharpe developed the Single Index Model (SIM),[42] which greatly reduces the number of computations, while preserving the essential E-V characteristics and accuracy of the Markowitz framework. For example, a 100-stock portfolio takes nearly 5,150 estimates of parameters using the Markowitz equations, whereas Sharpe's SIM needs only 302 such estimates. In Sharpe's SIM each security's return is related to a common denominator—namely, a market index, such as the Standard & Poor's 500—to which all common stocks can be related.

The computational problem is thus reduced to a simple regression analysis of any security being considered for a portfolio. Mathematically, the relationship is given by:

$$R_i = a_i + b_i \, (M) + e \qquad \text{(Equation 3)}$$

where:

R_i is the estimated return on stock i

a_i and b_i are regression constants (coefficients)

M relates to the market index, and

e is an error term whose expected value is zero.

Graphically, the relationship can be portrayed as follows:

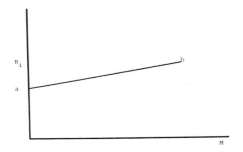

For each stock the graph shows the estimated return (R_i) for movements in the market level (M), and the beta coefficient (slope of the line) indicates the sensitivity of the movement of an individual stock to changes in the level of a common index (S&P 500). Alpha (a) indicates the estimated returns independent of the market index. Assume the following: alpha is 3 per cent, the beta coefficient is 1.2 (i.e., moves up or down 20 per cent faster than the market index), and e is zero; then, if the market moves up 10 per cent, this result follows:

$$R_i = 3\% + 1.2 \,(10\%) + 0 = 15\%$$

Beta is nearly always a positive coefficient, because most securities are positively corrrelated with the market. A few stocks, such as gold stocks, are negatively correlated and for this reason have much diversification potential in portfolios.

At this point, an important assumption is made in portfolio theory: as stocks are combined into portfolios, the alphas cancel to zero, leaving only betas; with the effect that such portfolios are considered efficient. Sharpe concludes:

> We reach, then, the key result of the efficient market theory. A security that is priced correctly will have an ex-ante alpha of zero in the eyes of well-informed analysts. And in an efficient market, all securities are priced correctly.[43]

Consequently, investors in an efficient market can select the betas they desire on portfolios. With the alphas canceled, portfolios would look like this:

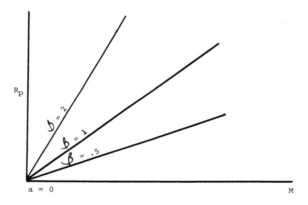

This means that portfolios become the weighted average of the individual securities' betas (each is being weighted by the proportion of portfolio funds invested in that stock), thus greatly simplifying the computational complexities found earlier in the Markowitz model. The Sharpe algorithm is thus an important advance in the practical handling of the risk-return characteristics of the large portfolios typical of institutional investors.

The Markowitz model and Sharpe algorithm suggest that the only relevant risk of an individual security in a portfolio context is its "systematic risk," measured by its beta value. If the alphas are eliminated by diversification, then, assuming an efficient market, investors should not be compensated for bearing unsystematic risk. Systematic risk for an individual security, or a portfolio, reflects market risk only; it is measured by beta and cannot be eliminated by diversification. Unsystematic risk reflects the unique risk of a security (the province of the security analyst)—those risks unique to the company and independent of the market. Unsystematic risk is measured by alpha and, for an efficient portfolio falling on the efficient frontier, can be completely eliminated by optimal diversification. Sharpe says, "A security's beta with respect to the overall market is the single most important measure of its risk. . . ."[44] This theory is addressed in Part IV-Question 9 of the Questionnaire.

Capital Asset Pricing Model (CAPM) [45]

The Capital Asset Pricing Model (CAPM) is a theory of competitive equilibrium in capital markets; it asserts that the appropriate pricing of the risk-return tradeoff of securities is a function of systematic risk and a risk-free (R_f) asset. Using Sharpe's Single Index Model (SIM) and the Markowitz framework, one can depict the CAPM as follows:

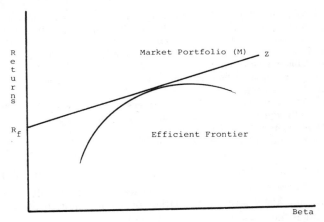

The graph shows that the equilibrium pricing of any stock or portfolio of stocks lies on the RMZ line (curve), and that this line dominates all portfolios on the efficient frontier except the market portfolio (which in principle is the market value index of all stocks or risky assets weighted by their capitalizations). This means that the expected return of an individual asset or portfolio of assets is a linear function of beta, with the mathematical form of:

$$E\ (R_i)\ =\ a\ +\ bB_i$$

where:

$a\ =\ R_f$ (risk-free asset)

$b\ =\ E\ (R_M) - R_f$ (expected returns on the market portfolio less the value of the risk-free asset)

Marshall E. Blume and Irwin Friend state that:

> Since the coefficients a and b are independent of asset i, [the equation above] should, according to the market-line theory (CAPM), hold for any individual asset as well as any portfolio of assets. Any departure from [the equation above] would be inconsistent with the market-line theory.[46]

The Capital Asset Pricing Model in its most rigorous form is based on a number of restrictive and simplifying assumptions. Michael C. Jensen enumerated these as follows:

1. All investors have single-period time horizon and attempt to maximize their expected utility of terminal wealth by choosing among alternative portfolios on the basis of mean and variance of returns.
2. Unlimited lending and borrowing opportunities at risk free rate of interest is available to all investors.
3. All investors have identical expectations of means, variances, and covariances of all security returns.
4. The capital markets are perfect in the sense that all assets are perfectly divisible, perfectly liquid, there are no transactions costs and taxes.
5. All investors are price takers.
6. The quantities of all assets are known.[47]

A controversial assumption of the CAPM is the role of the risk-free asset. It asserts that investors can build an optimal portfolio by a combination of the risk-free asset and risky assets (the market portfolio), and further, can either borrow or lend at the risk-free rate, as depicted below:

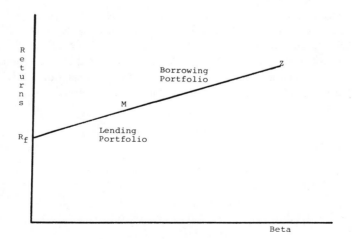

In principle, if the investor wants a portfolio that perfectly tracks the market portfolio, he will invest in a representative sample of stocks (S&P 500) that, by definition, gives a beta of 1. In other words, he invests in an Index Fund. If he prefers a less risky portfolio, he can combine the risk-free asset (with beta = 0) in any proportion with the market portfolio or Index Fund (with beta = 1) to arrive at the desired beta (risk). For example, if he wants a beta of .5, then the funds are divided equally between the risk-free asset and the Index Fund. This is called a lending portfolio. If he wants a beta of 2, he can borrow one-half the funds (e.g., use a 50 per cent margin account) and place them entirely in the Index Fund, thus leveraging the portfolio to a beta of 2.

Since the Capital Asset Pricing Model asserts that the investor cannot make expected returns greater than the risks assumed and that any portfolio in equilibrium will lie on the market line (curve R_fMZ), the investor can as easily use a passive interest strategy of an Index Fund (i.e., an "unmanaged fund") in desired combination with the risk-free asset (Part IV-Question 10). Some large institutional investors have adopted this passive strategy.

Criticisms of the Capital Asset Pricing Model usually concern the restrictive and unrealistic nature of its assumptions. A number of tests of the CAPM have been made to determine its robustness, even when various assumptions are relaxed with the intention of making them more realistic. Important empirical studies of the CAPM have been made by Jacob;[48] Miller and Scholes;[49] Friend and Blume;[50] Black, Jensen, and Scholes;[51] Fama and McBeth;[52] Lintner;[53] Levy;[54] and others. In general, the empirical tests indicate that the CAPM holds up reasonably well when large portfolios are examined, but fails to predict or explain the risk-return behavior of individual assets. According to Franco Modigliani and Gerald R. Pogue,[55] the principal results from testing the CAPM are:

1. The evidence shows a significant positive relationship between realized returns and systematic risk. However, the slope of the relationship (beta) is usually less than predicted by the Capital Asset Pricing Model.

2. The relationship between risk and return appears to be linear. The studies give no evidence of significant curvature in the risk-return relationship.

3. Tests that attempt to discriminate between the effects of systematic and unsystematic risk do not yield definitive results. Both kinds of risk appear to be positively related to security returns. However, there is substantial support for the proposition that the relationship between return and unsystematic risk is at least partly spurious—that is, partly reflecting statistical problems rather than the true nature of capital markets.

5

Methodology and Results of Questionnaire

Data for this research project were collected by mailed questionnaire conducted during June 26-July 28, 1978. Questionnaires were sent to all National Investor Relations Institute (NIRI) members who were associated with corporations, regardless of title within the organization. No outside counselors were sent questionnaires. A pre-addressed, pre-paid return envelope was provided each individual.

It was believed that the NIRI members constitute a sample within themselves, since all public corporation must perform disclosure functions. The questionnaire was limited to NIRI members in order to obtain a better response rate. It was thought that the NIRI members would be more familiar with corporate policies and objectives relating to disclosure than would others in the organizational structure.

A second questionnaire, similar to the NIRI questionnaire, was mailed to a group of security analysts. The analysts chosen were all Chartered Financial Analysts (CFAs), associated with the sell-side (i.e., with investment banking or securities firms), who were listed in the 1978 CFA Membership Directory as having a primary job function of company analysis. This classification and screening process produced 560 analysts; 318 of these were based in New York City, and the remainder were from other cities in the United States and Canada. CFAs were chosen because it was believed that these analysts would have more knowledge of, and be most familiar with: (1) corporate investor relations programs, (2) information needs of investors, and (3) modern investment theory literature. A pre-addressed and pre-paid return envelope was provided each CFA.

The two questionnaires sent are presented on the following pages.

DESCRIPTION OF THE QUESTIONNAIRE

The questionnaire is divided into four parts. Althoughs Parts I and II are similar for both NIRI and CFAs, they are not exactly the same. Parts III and IV are identical for both groups.

QUESTIONNAIRE 1

Dear Investor Relations Specialist:

This questionnaire is designed to gain insight into the investor relations activities of your company, and your attitude toward: (a) security analysts as an investment audience; (b) certain kinds of information being disclosed by corporations to investors, and (c) certain ideas now being taught in graduate business schools as "modern investment theory."

Your cooperation is strongly solicited, as the questionnaire results will form the basis for my Ph.D. dissertation at the University of Arkansas, entitled "The Corporate Investor Relations Function: A Survey of Activities and Attitudes." Your answers will remain completely confidential. Only total results of the survey will be disclosed in the dissertation. The questionnaire is coded so that additional information can be obtained, if needed, from conventional sources (e.g., Moody's or Standard & Poor's) to implement the survey results.

Please furnish the information requested, and mark the scales which reflect your attitude or opinion. Please return the questionnaire in the enclosed envelope, addressed to my supervising professor, by July 28. My Ph.D. depends on the timing and quality of your answers. I need your help! Thank you.

Mollie H. Wilson

PART I

1. List the principal goals or objectives of   –
   your company's investor relations program.   –
   –
   –

Circle or check the answer which most adequately describes your company.

2. Overall, how well has your company
   achieved the goals you listed in the
   past few years?

   | Not at all | Poorly | Average | Fairly Well | Very Well |

3. Some companies are more active in seeking
   investor recognition in relevant investment
   markets. How would you characterize your
   company's investor relations program in
   this respect?

   | Very Passive | Moder. Passive | Neutral | Moder. Active | Highly Active |

4. More specifically, in your efforts to cultivate a following by security analysts, how
   would you characterize your company's
   investor relations program?

   | Very Passive | Moder. Passive | Neutral | Moder. Active | Highly Active |

5. If you believe you are more active than
   other companies in seeking investor   –
   recognition, please enumerate 2 or 3   –
   examples of this increased effort.   –
   –

6. Is the market performance of your
   stock important to your company as
   a corporate objective?

No Importance	Average Importance	Great Importance

7. In viewing the performance of your
   company's stock in the marketplace,
   how would you rate it?

	Substan. Under- valued	Moder. Under- valued	Fully Priced	Moder. Over- valued	Substan. Over- valued
a. Currently	————	————	———	————	————
b. Overall, during the past 12 months	————	————	———	————	————
c. Overall, during the past 5 years	————	————	———	————	————

* The term "undervalued" refers to the Graham and Dodd idea of a stock trading in the
marketplace at less than its "intrinsic" or "central" value. Conversely, "overvalued" means a
stock traded in the marketplace at more than its "intrinsic" value.

8. Overall, do you believe your investor
   relations program has had an impact
   on the market price of your company's
   stock?

Unfavorable Impact	No Impact	Favorable Impact

9. In terms of your investor relations
   effort, what do you do, if anything, to
   influence the price of your company's
   stock?

———————————————————————
———————————————————————
———————————————————————
———————————————————————

10. Does your firm have formal, written
    policies for investor relations?

Yes ————   No ————

PART II

This section pertains to your overall assessment of security analysts that follow your
company.

1. How many security analysts follow your
   company on a *regular* basis?

———————————————————————

2. How many security analysts follow your
   company on an *irregular*, or less frequent,
   basis?

———————————————————————

3. Please evaluate the security analysts who
   follow your company on a *regular* basis,
   giving your overall assessment of how well
   they have performed in the following areas:

	1 Very Poorly	2 Below Average	3 Average	4 Above Average	5 Very Well
A. Understanding the nature of your business?	1	2	3	4	5
B. Understanding the operating and financial risks of your business	1	2	3	4	5

C. Estimating your future earnings	1	2	3	4	5
D. Estimating the value of your stock	1	2	3	4	5

4. How many analysts, who follow your company on a *regular* basis, do an excellent overall job of evaluating your company?   _____

5. How many analysts, who follow your company on a *regular* basis, do a very poor overall job of evaluating your company?   _____

PART III

Please circle whether you agree or disagree with the following types of information as being helpful in investment decision-making (whether or not required by the SEC).	1 Strongly Disagree	2 Moder. Disagree	3 Neutral	4 Moder. Agree	5 Strongly Agree
1. Business segment (line of business) reporting	1	2	3	4	5
2. Leases capitalized on the balance sheet	1	2	3	4	5
3. Footnotes written in "plain English" to assist the small investor in understanding the financial statements	1	2	3	4	5
4. Auditor involvement (participation) in quarterly reports	1	2	3	4	5
5. Explicit disclosure of auditors' fees	1	2	3	4	5
6. Explicit supplementary disclosure of investor relations costs for the past year (similar to disclosure of advertising and R&D expenses)	1	2	3	4	5
7. Replacement cost information	1	2	3	4	5
8. Dividend policy, stated in terms of payout ratio (point estimate or range)	1	2	3	4	5
9. Capital expenditures planned for the next 12 months	1	2	3	4	5
10. Target debt-equity ratio to be maintained in future years	1	2	3	4	5

11. Management forecast of sales (point or
    range) for next 12 months   1   2   3   4   5

12. Management forecast of earnings (point or
    range) for next 12 months   1   2   3   4   5

13. Management forecast of earnings per share
    (point or range) for next 12 months   1   2   3   4   5

14. More information is now being required
    of corporations by the SEC than is necessary
    to ensure efficient capital markets   1   2   3   4   5

15. Please list any information (either "hard" or "soft," historical or forward-looking) that
    you believe corporations should furnish, but are not now disclosing, that would be
    helpful in investment decision-making: ------------------------------
    ----

PART IV

*Over the past decade or so, developments in investment theory have led to the academic
view, sometimes called the "efficient markets hypothesis," that capital markets in the
United States are "efficient" in the sense that: (a) security prices react rapidly to new information, and that (b) investors will be unable to earn extraordinarily high rates of return on
securities. This view is now being taught in graduate business schools. However, there are
numerous investment groups, notably practitioners, who do not necessarily share these
academic views.*

Please circle the extent you agree or disagree with the following academic views:	1 Strongly Disagree	2 Moder. Disagree	3 Neutral	4 Moder. Agree	5 Strongly Agree

1. Security price changes are random and
   unpredictable (i.e., they form a
   "random walk")   1   2   3   4   5

2. Knowledge of historical patterns of
   stock prices (work of the "chartists")
   does not aid investors in attaining
   improved investment performance   1   2   3   4   5

3. Publicly available information on
   securities is quickly discounted by
   the securities market   1   2   3   4   5

4. Stock prices at any point in time will
   represent good estimates of intrinsic
   or fundamental values   1   2   3   4   5

5. Apart from any cash dividend effects, a
    stock split increases the total value of
    the corporation's shares outstanding
    because investors are more inclined
    to purchase lower priced securities   1   2   3   4   5

6. "Good news" is disseminated to the
    market more promptly by corporations
    than "bad news"   1   2   3   4   5

7. Most published security analysis is
    logically incomplete and valueless   1   2   3   4   5

8. There are more security analysts than
    are needed to keep the stock market
    efficient   1   2   3   4   5

9. Beta, as a measure of "systematic risk"
    (which measures the sensitivity of
    movements in individual stocks to the
    movements in a relevant market index
    such as the S&P 500), is the single most
    important measure of a security's risk   1   2   3   4   5

10. The use of index funds, called "indexing"
    (such as simulating the S&P 500) is
    the prudent way for large institutional
    investors to invest their funds in
    common stocks   1   2   3   4   5

11. Have you had exposure to these academic
    ideas, either by reading or by experience?   Not at
    (Circle one)   All   Some   A Lot

12. In the past few years, have statements
    such as those above affected the way
    you perform your professional duties?   Not at
    (Circle one)   All   Some   A Lot

        If your job has been affected, please
        give examples: _____
                                _____
                                _____
                                _____

QUESTIONNAIRE 2

Dear C.F.A.:

This questionnaire is designed to gain insight into the investor relations activities of the companies you follow, and your attitude toward: (a) the effectiveness of corporate investor relations program; (b) certain kinds of information being disclosed by corporations to investors; and (c) certain ideas now being taught in graduate business schools as "modern investment theory."

Your cooperation is strongly solicited, as the questionnaire results will form the basis for my Ph.D. dissertation at the University of Arkansas, entitled "The Corporate Investor Relations Function: Survey of Activities and Attitudes." Your answers will remain completely confidential. Only total results of the survey will be disclosed in the dissertation.

Pleasure furnish the information requested, and mark the scales which reflect your attitude or opinion. Please return the questionnaire in the enclosed envelope, addressed to my supervising professor, by July 28. My Ph.D. depends on the timing and quality of your answers. I need your help!

Thank you,

Mollie H. Wilson

PART I

1. What is your title?

2. What year did you receive the CFA designation?

3. What is your highest academic degree?

   - In what field?

4. What do you believe should be the principal goals and objectives of the investor relations programs of those companies you follow on a regular basis (i.e., those companies where you have personal contact with management?)

Please circle the answer which most adequately describes the investor relations programs of the companies you regularly follow.

5. Overall, how well have the companies you follow achieved the investor relations goals you listed during the past year?

   Not at All   Poorly   Average   Fairly Well   Very Well

6. Some companies are more active in seeking investor recognition in relevant

investment markets. How would you characterize the investor relations programs of the companies you follow?

| Very Passive | Moder. Passive | Neutral | Moder. Active | Very Active |

7. More specifically, in their efforts to cultivate a following by security analysts, how would you characterize their efforts?

| Very Passive | Moder. Passive | Neutral | Moder. Active | Very Active |

8. Concerning the companies you follow, should the market performance of these stocks be important to the investor relations efforts of the companies?

| No Importance | Average Importance | Great Importance |

9. Overall, do you believe that investor relations programs of these companies have had an impact on their market prices?

| Unfavorable Impact | No Impact | Favorable Impact |

10. In terms of their corporate investor relations efforts, what should these companies do, if anything, to influence the performance of their stock?

———————————————————————
———————————————————————
———————————————————————
———————————————————————

11. In your opinion, do you believe an active investor relations program has an effect on the market performance of a company's stock?

| Unfavorable Effect | No Effect | Favorable Effect |

PART II

This section pertains to your overall assessment of investor relations programs of the companies you regularly follow:

1. How many companies do you follow on a *regular* basis? (companies where you have personal contact with management)

———————————————————————

   - On an *irregular,* or less frequent, basis?

———————————————————————

2. Please circle how well the companies you follow on a *regular* basis have done in directly supplying you information that allows you to:

| 1 Very Poorly | 2 Below Average | 3 Average | 4 Above Average | 5 Very Well |

  A. Understand the nature of their business

| 1 | 2 | 3 | 4 | 5 |

  B. Understand the operating and financial risk of their business

| 1 | 2 | 3 | 4 | 5 |

C. Estimate their future earnings   1   2   3   4   5

D. Estimate the value of their stock   1   2   3   4   5

E. How would you rate their candor
in communicating and discussing
negative developments?   1   2   3   4   5

3. How many of the companies you follow
on a *regular* basis have an excellent investor relations program?   _____

4. How many of the companies you follow
on a *regular* basis have a very poor investor relations program?   _____

PART III

Please circle whether you agree or disagree with the following types of information as being helpful in investment decision-making (whether or not required by the SEC).	1 Strongly Disagree	2 Moder. Disagree	3 Neutral	4 Moder. Agree	5 Strongly Agree
1. Business segment (line of business) reporting	1	2	3	4	5
2. Leases capitalized on the balance sheet	1	2	3	4	5
3. Footnotes written in "plain English" to assist the small investor in understanding the financial statements	1	2	3	4	5
4. Auditor involvement (participation) in quarterly reports	1	2	3	4	5
5. Explicit disclosure of auditors' fees	1	2	3	4	5
6. Explicit supplementary disclosure of investor relations costs for the past year (similar to disclosure of advertising and R&D expenses)	1	2	3	4	5
7. Replacement cost information	1	2	3	4	5
8. Dividend policy, stated in terms of payout ratio (point estimate or range)	1	2	3	4	5
9. Capital expenditures planned for the next 12 months	1	2	3	4	5
10. Target debt-equity ratio to be maintained in future years	1	2	3	4	5

11. Management forecast of sales (point or
    range) for next 12 months   1   2   3   4   5

12. Management forecast of earnings (point or
    range) for next 12 months   1   2   3   4   5

13. Management forecast of earnings per share
    (point or range) for next 12 months   1   2   3   4   5

14. More information is now being required of
    corporations by the SEC than is necessary
    to ensure efficient capital markets   1   2   3   4   5

15. Please list any information (either "hard" or
    "soft," historical or forward-looking) that   — — — — — — — — — — — — — — — —
    you believe corporations should furnish,   — — — — — — — — — — — — — — — —
    but are not now disclosing, that would be   — — — — — — — — — — — — — — — —
    helpful in investment decision-making: — — — — — — — — — — — — — — — —

PART IV

Over the past decade or so, developments in investment theory have led to the academic view, sometimes called the "efficient markets hypothesis," that capital markets in the United States are "efficient" in the sense that: (a) security prices react rapidly to new information, and that (b) investors will be unable to earn extraordinarily high rates of return on securities. This view is now being taught in graduate business schools. However, there are numerous investment groups, notably practitioners, who do not necessarily share these academic views.

Please circle the extent you agree or disagree with the following academic views:	Strongly Disagree	Moder. Disagree	Neutral	Moder. Agree	Strongly Agree
1. Security price changes are random and unpredictable (i.e., they form a "random walk").	1	2	3	4	5
2. Knowledge of historical patterns of stock prices (work of the "chartists") does not aid investors in attaining improved investment performance	1	2	3	4	5
3. Publicly available information on securities is quickly discounted by the securities market	1	2	3	4	5
4. Stock prices at any point in time will represent good estimates of intrinsic or fundament values	1	2	3	4	5

5. Apart from any cash dividend effects, a stock
   split increases the total value of the

corporation's shares outstanding because
investors are more inclined to purchase
lower priced securities   1   2   3   4   5

6. "Good news" is disseminated to the
    market more promptly by corporations
    than "bad news"   1   2   3   4   5

7. Most published security analysis is
    logically incomplete and valueless   1   2   3   4   5

8. There are more security analysts than are
    needed to keep the stock market efficient 1   2   3   4   5

9. Beta, as a measure of "systematic risk"
    (which measures the sensitivity of move-
    ments in individual stocks to the movements
    in a relevant market index such as the S&P
    500) is the single most important measure
    of a security's risk.   1   2   3   4   5

10. The use of index funds, called "indexing"
    (such as simulating the S&P 500) is the
    prudent way for large institutional
    investors to invest their funds in common
    stocks.   1   2   3   4   5

11. Have you had exposure to these academic
    ideas, either by reading or by experience? Not
    (Circle one answer)   at All   Some   A Lot

12. In the past few years, have statements
    such as those above affected the way you   Not
    perform your professional duties?   at All   Some   A Lot
    (Circle one answer)

    -   If your job has been affected, please
        give examples: _____
                                              _____
                                              _____
                                              _____

Part I

Part I on the NIRI questionnaire consists of 10 questions. Part I on the CFA questionnaire consists of 11 questions, including 3 questions of background information. The NIRI questionnaire does not include questions about background, as the National NIRI Headquarters had sent a background questionnaire to corporate members during June, 1978, and the surveyor was told that the questionnaire and results would be available for inclusion in this study. Some of the relevant results are included in Chapter 2. Part I attempts to determine the goals and objectives of the investor relations program, as viewed by both the internal investor relations specialist and the outside analyst, and to evaluate how well these stated goals and objectives have been achieved, Part I also examines the perceived level of activity of the investor relations programs, and the apparent relation of these programs to corporate stock price movements.

Part II

Part II requests from the company the number of analysts who follow the company on both a regular and an irregular basis; from the analyst, it requests the number of companies he follows on both a regular and an irregular basis.

Part II also requests that the internal investor relations specialist rate the analysts who follow his company; the analyst in turn is requested to rate the quality and quantity of information provided by the company he is following. Part II has five questions for the NIRI member and four for the CFA.

Part III

Part III contains 15 questions. The overall purpose of this section is to ask both groups to comment on the information currently required by the SEC, and some that is not presently required but is considered potentially useful in investment decision-making. Finally, both groups are asked if they believe that more information is now being required of corporations than is necessary to ensure efficient capital markets. Both groups also are asked to list any information which corporations should furnish but which is not now being disclosed, that would be helpful in investment decision-making.

Part IV

Part IV asks 10 questions relating to modern investment theory. The purpose of this section is to determine whether either group is familiar with, and agrees with, modern investment theory. The final question asks if this theory has affected the way the respondents perform their jobs, and if so, to give examples.

QUESTIONNAIRE PRE-TEST

After the original questionnaire was developed, it was pre-tested. The original questionnaire was quite different from the final forms. Members of the Arkansas Society of Financial Managers were used as the pre-test sample. After completion of the questionnaire, personal interviews were held to determine why respondents answered as they did. Each volunteer also was asked to time and comment on the questionnaire, and to make suggestions for improvement, especially with regard to word clarification. A majority of the volunteers took approximately 10 minutes to answer the questionnaire. As a result of this pre-test, several headings were changed, and some questions were reworded.

TESTS OF HYPOTHESES

For the statistical analysis, the SAS-76 program system was used.[1] The chi-square test was selected as an appropriate descriptive statistic. The chi-square is appropriate to determine if there are significant differences between two independent groups when the data are composed of frequencies or discrete categories and the measurement is at least nominal. The hypothesis tested by chi-square is that the two groups differ "with respect to the relative frequency with which the group members fall in several categories."[2] In this study, therefore, the SAS program FREQ procedure created various frequency and cross-tabulation tables to test the questionnaire hypotheses. An alpha level of .05 was selected as the probability level at or below which the research hypotheses would be accepted.

LIMITATIONS

As with any research project, certain limitations result from the research methodology. In general, these limitations relate to: (1) the scope and the research and the generalization of the results, based upon the sample chosen for study; (2) the nature of the concepts to be measured; (3) the method of data collection; and (4) the constraints of time and financial resources.[3] The limitation of external validity is related to the scope of the research and generalization of the results beyond the sample chosen for study. In this research project, the sample was taken from two groups whose job-related functions call for familiarity with SEC disclosure requirements, and valuation methods for stock.

Another limitation is the method of data collection. By using a mailed questionnaire, the researcher loses control once the questionnaire is mailed.

One of the problems inherent in mailed questionnaires is the possibility of less than satisfactory response rates. Respondent cooperation is voluntary, of course, and a large percentage return is unusual. Because of the relatively large response rate of these questionnaires, however, a follow-up mailing was not considered necessary.

The validity of the measurement is a limitation of the study. The questionnaire was designed to seek responses to questions which were related to a theoretical framework. A problem with the questionnaire was that the researcher needed to be sure that all respondents interpreted the questions the same way. Based upon results of the pre-tests it appeared that all respondents did interpret the questionnaire as desired.

Another aspect associated with validity is whether each respondent interpreted the response scales similarly. No test was made to determine if the scale was interpreted equally by respondents. Scales were clearly labeled so that the potential for varying interpretations was minimized.

DESCRIPTION OF CHI-SQUARE (X^2)

The statistical test for significance used for the majority of questions was the chi-square test; it is designated as X^2. The chi-square test is a general test of significance to indicate if a significant number of the survey respondents answered differently from the other survey group. The basic (null) hypothesis is that no difference is expected; so the alternative hypothesis is that a significant difference is detectable. The chi-square test looks at the difference between the observed frequencies (O) and the expected frequencies (E). Since no difference is necessarily expected, the difference between the observed and expected frequencies should be small. If the groups' responses are different, a large difference between the observed and expected frequencies should exist. The problem then becomes one of the researcher's determining how large a difference is large enough to be considered "statistically significant."

With Question 13, Part III of the Questionnaire as an example, the test is defined as follows:

	Lo	Hi	n_i
NIRI	95	90	185
CFA	50	117	147
c_j	125	207	332 respondents

E_j = expected = $n_i c_j/n$ O = observed

$$E_{11} = 185 \times 125 / 332 = 69.65$$
$$E_{12} = 185 \times 207 / 332 = 115.35$$
$$E_{21} = 147 \times 125 / 332 = 55.35$$
$$E_{22} = 147 \times 207 / 332 = 91.65$$

$$T = \sum_i \sum_j \frac{(O - E)^2}{E}$$

$$T = \frac{(95 - 69.65)^2}{69.65} \qquad \frac{(90 - 115.35)^2}{115.35} \qquad \frac{(30 - 55.35)^2}{55.35} \qquad \frac{(117 - 91.65)^2}{91.65}$$

$$= \quad 9.23 \quad + \quad 5.57 \qquad 11.60 \qquad 7.01$$

$$= \quad 33.41$$

T (computational formula) $= \dfrac{N(0_4 0_{22} - 0_{12} 0_{21})^2}{n_1 n_2 c_1 c_2}$

$$= \frac{332 (95 \times 17 - 90 \times 30)^2}{185 \times 147 \times 125 \times 207}$$

$$= \quad 33.41$$

$X^2_{(.95, 1)} = 3.84$

$33.41 > 3.84$

H_0 = There is no difference between the CFAs and NIRI, in the way the groups marked Question 13, Part III.

H_a = There is a statistical difference between the CFAs and the NIRIs, in the way the groups marked Question 13, Part III.

$33.41 > 3.84$; Therefore, reject the null hypothesis (H_0) and accept the alternate (H_a).

Based on the computer program used, the printout gives the chi-square score, degrees of freedom, and probability (level of significance) for each question examined. Any time the probability is scored at .05 or less, the null hypothesis (H_0) of no difference is rejected; otherwise its alternative (H_a) is accepted.

Optionally, as in the foregoing illustration, where $X^2 > 3.84$ (which in this case is 33.41), the null hypothesis is rejected, and the alternative hypothesis is accepted.

DESCRIPTION OF HI-LO TEST

The Hi-Lo procedure is a method to regroup the data into two opinion groups rather than the five that was the usual scale in this questionnaire. With the Hi-Lo procedure, if a significant difference was shown between the NIRI and CFA in the way they marked the data, a chi-square test could be used to determine whether one group was significantly higher or lower than the other group.

The five categories were grouped first with Cells 1 and 2 as "Lo" and Cells 3, 4, and 5 as "Hi". The 2 x 2 chi-square test statistic was calculated. The regrouping placed Cells 1, 2, and 3 as "Lo" and Cells 4 and 5 as "Hi." The test statistic was again calculated. The test statistic need to be large enough to be significant both ways, i.e., significant even when calculated the most conservative way in the regrouping. Therefore, only when the data were weighted against rejection of the null hypothesis and the difference was still significantly large, was the NIRI or CFA declared to be either higher or lower than the other.

CHAPTER ORGANIZATIONAL PLAN

In the balance of this chapter, the survey findings are, first, quantitatively presented in summary tables for each question, or for paired sets of questions, in the four parts of the questionnaire. Each summary table is followed by the statistical significance of the results, which shows the chi-square values, the degrees of freedom, and the probability coefficient with respect to accepting/rejecting the null hypothesis centered around the .05 level of significance.

Under each table are appropriate comments summarizing and interpreting the results of this research project. Usually, this discussion covers the overall conclusion of the table, any of its salient features in the results, and the acceptance/rejection of the null hypothesis (H_0). In the discussion, the percentages are rounded off to the nearest whole number so as to avoid the appearance of "spurious accuracy."

When justified, another table is presented sequentially following the original table that summarizes the Hi-Lo results. Also, results from the correlation analysis and multi-way contingency tables are presented for selected groups of questions. The computational details are too voluminous to be presented, but are available on request.

Finally, the general summary, conclusions, and implications of the overall results, as well as summary conclusions to each question contained in the questionnaire, are reserved for Chapter 6.

PART I

CFA I-1, 2, 3   CFA Profile*

What is your title?

CFAs classified as:		No.
1. Operating security analyst		73
2. Holding joint executive titles		65
3. Corporate finance and other		8
	Total	146

Year CFA was granted?

1. 1963-1968		41
2. 1969-1975		54
3. 1976-1977		50
	Total	145

Highest academic degree?

1. Bachelor's		38
2. Master's		98
3. Ph.D. and other		4
	Total	140

---

* CFA I-1, 2, 3 refers to the CFA section of the Questionnaire, Part I-Questions 1, 2, and 3. All tables are similarly coded to the Questionnaire.

These three questions were designed to elicit a statistical profile of the CFAs with respect to: (1) job classification; (2) when the CFA was obtained by grouped years; (3) academic background. Comparable information was obtained on the NIRI group from a 1973 survey, and the updated version of this survey conducted in the summer of 1978 is included in Chapter 2.

The survey results clearly indicate that the CFAs have operating responsibility to analyze companies and industries and to pass their recommendations on to final users (investors). Almost half of these analysts (46 per cent) hold executive positions in their respective investment banking and brokerage firms, which suggests that they have the additional responsibilities of supervising the analytical work of their analyst staffs. Therefore, as a group, they interface operationally with the public corporations they follow, as well as to assume, in about half the cases, executive responsibility within their respective firms.

The grouped years within which the analysts received the CFA designation were selected so that about equal numbers could be assessed. First, the survey results show that, as time progressed, an ever larger number sat for, and were granted, the CFA certification. Second, the grouped years (except 1976-1977) cover full business cycles. Third, there has been an evolution from 1963 on, with a tightening of the standards and an altering of the coverage of the CFA exams, with growing emphasis on modern investment theory.

A conclusion of this study (not presented because of its voluminous nature, but available on request) is that there is a slight but discernible trend for the 1976-1977 CFAs to reject modern investment theory (Part IV of the questionnaire) to a slightly lesser extent than their older peer groups (1963-1968; 1969-1971). The reason is clear: they have had more recent and intensive exposure, at college and in the CFA exams, to modern investment theory. However, it is important to recognize that even they, as a group, continue to reject what they were taught in college.

Finally, the survey results show a large majority of the CFAs holding their master's degree (70 per cent) and most of them in business administration or its equivalent. In this context, the CFAs are generally a highly educated group, which also is bound to the high professional and ethical standards set by the ICFA. It can be concluded, without equivocation, that the survey sample indicates a group of educated, skilled, and professionally certified security analysts, and that it does, indeed, constitute the elite in the Financial Analyst Federation's membership of over 14,000 security analysts.

IR I-1 :   List the principal goals or objectives of your company's investor relations program

1.	Provide solid understanding of company–fair valuation	57
2.	Maintain *fair* stock price	40
3.	Increased investment community interest	31
4.	Communication to keep investment community informed	29
5.	Broaden (diversify) shareholder base	26
6.	Increase price-earnings ratio, maximize stock price	16
7.	Meet needs of, and provide information to shareholders	14
8.	Increased investor loyalty	8
9.	Improve, maintain liquidity (trading volume)	11
10.	Fulfill legal requirements	4
11.	Involve management	4
12.	Maintain, promote "quality" image	3
13.	Increase institutional ownership	3
14.	Personal contact with analysts	1
15.	Provide an orderly market for stock	1
16.	Meet financial reporting requirements	1
		249

CFA I-4:   What do you believe should be the principal goals and objectives of the investor relations programs of those companies you follow on a regular basis?

1.	Dissemination of information ("timely," "reliable")	84
2.	Make business understandable: provide insight, interpretation, explain corporate philosophy	26
3.	Honest, unbiased and balanced (both positive and negative) view of company	18
4.	Opening up "access" to management, insight into management philosophy	14
5.	Inform shareholders specifically	8
6.	Forewarn financial community of significant new developments, fundamental changes in business	7
7.	Provide reliable contact for inquiries	7
8.	High stock prices (stability, also)	5
9.	Promote interest in company	3
10.	Access for all analysts	3
11.	Facilitate raising of (and lower cost of) capital	2
12.	Explicate future plans and goals	2
13.	Make management comments meaningful	1
14.	Understand economic role of company	1
15.	Minimize "random" fluctuations in stock price	1
16.	Be fully knowledgeable about company	1
17.	Understand economic role of company	1
18.	Don't know	1
		182

IR I-2:   How well has your company achieved the goals you listed during the past
few years?

CFA I-5:   How well have the companies you follow achieved the investor relations
goals you listed during the past year?

		1 Not at All	2 Poorly	3 Average	4 Fairly Well	5 Very Well	Totals
NIRI	Frequency Per Cent	—	12 6.45	36 19.35	91 48.92	47 25.27	186
CFA	Frequency Per Cent	—	13 8.84	34 23.13	85 57.82	15 10.20	147
TOTALS	Frequency Per Cent	—	25 7.51	70 21.02	176 52.85	62 18.62	333

Chi-Square = 12.421   DF = 4   Prob = .0061

There was a significant difference in the way members of the NIRI and the CFAs answered this question. The chi-square probability was 0.0061; however, when tested on the Hi-Lo scale, no significant difference showed. A visual check of the table on the 1-5 scale shows the difference in the marking of the 5 Cell (Very Well), with NIRI members giving a "5" answer approximately 25 per cent of the time, and the CFAs believing that the companies they follow achieve their investor relations goals very well only about 10 per cent of the time. This appears to be a normal bias, since the NIRI members would tend to rate themselves higher in their goal achievement. Overall, both groups appear satisfied that the appropriate investor relations objectives are being achieved.

IR I-3:   Some companies are more active in seeking investor recognition in relevant investment markets. How would you characterize your company's investor relations program in this respect?

CFA I-6:   How would you characterize the investor relations programs of the companies you follow?

		1 Very Passive	2 Moder. Passive	3 Neutral	4 Moder. Active	5 Highly Active	Totals
NIRI	Frequency	3	20	22	101	39	185
	Per Cent	1.62	10.81	11.89	54.59	21.08	
CFA	Frequency	1	10	23	89	21	144
	Per Cent	.69	6.94	15.97	61.81	14.58	
TOTALS	Frequency	4	30	45	190	60	329
	Per Cent	1.22	9.12	13.68	57.75	18.24	

Chi-Square = 5.489   DF = 4   Prob. = .2407

There is no significant difference in the way the two groups answered this question, either on the 1-5 scale, or the Hi-Lo scale. Both groups marked approximately 55-60 per cent in Cell 4 (Moderately Active), and this cell was the highest marked of any. The NIRIs marked Cell 5 (Highly Active) 20 per cent of the time, and the CFAs marked this cell only 15 per cent. However, this difference does not appear to be significant based on the chi-square probabilities, with four degrees of freedom. Both investor relations specialists and CFAs agree overall (76 per cent) that the investor relations programs are active.

IR I-2, 3:   Correlation between Question 2 and 3

	Question 3		
Question 2	0.16639	—	Correlation
	0.0240	—	Probability
	184	—	Total observations

The NIRIs responses indicated they felt their companies achieved their listed goals over the past few years fairly well to very well, and that most NIRI members characterize their companies' investor relations program as moderately active to very active. It was felt that an investigation into the correlation of these responses would be beneficial. Is the investor relations specialist who reports an active investor relations program the same one who reports attainment of listed goals?

At a statistical significance of .05, the Spearman's Rank Correlation values were significant. The positive correlation (0.16639) indicates that a low response on goal attainment would be paired with a low response on program activity, and correspondingly, a high response on goal attainment would be paired with a high response on the program activity. Thus, the null hypothesis is rejected in favor of the alternative, that there is significant difference.

IR I-4:   In your efforts to cultivate a following by security analysts, how would you characterize your company's investor relations program?

CFA I-7:   In their efforts to cultivate a following by security analysts, how would you characterize their efforts?

---

		1 Very Passive	2 Moder. passive	3 Neutral	4 Moder. Active	5 Highly Active	Totals
NIRI	Frequency	6	15	12	93	60	186
	Per Cent	3.23	8.06	6.45	50.00	32.26	
CFA	Frequency	–	12	22	91	20	145
	Per Cent		8.28	15.17	62.76	13.79	
TOTALS	Frequency	6	27	34	184	80	331
	Per Cent	1.81	8.16	10.27	55.59	24.17	

Chi-Square = 24.595   DF = 4   Prob. = 0.001

This table shows a significant difference on the 1-5 scale, between the way the NIRIs and CFAs marked, but the same difference is not apparent on the Hi-Lo table. From a visual inspection, the major difference appears to be the greater number of "5" answers (Highly Active) by NIRI respondents than by the CFAs. The NIRIs marked Cell 5 32 per cent of the time, while the CFAs marked Cell 5 only 13 per cent of the time. It should be noted that the NIRIs marked Cell 1 3 per cent, while no CFAs marked Cell 1 (Very Passive). At best this suggests that the CFAs expect some investor relations program to be in place before they even consider the company to be worth following. Both investor relations specialists (82 per cent) and CFAs (76 per cent) agree that companies have active programs to cultivate security analysts.

IR I-5:   Please give two or three examples of increased investor relations effort

---

		No.
1.	Analyst and/or broker meetings	67
2.	Individual calling programs on analysts and/or brokers	39
3.	Direct mailing programs of corporate/financial reports	19
4.	Preparation of factbooks and other corporate descriptive materials	14
5.	Make ourselves available to inquiries	8
6.	Corporate advertising	7
7.	Extensive reporting to interested individuals and institutions	7
8.	Line of business and other corporate data disclosure	6
9.	Telephone contacts with analysts and/or brokers	6
10.	Field trips	5
11.	More active than in the past	5
12.	High level of communications with existing shareholders	3
13.	Shareholder and analyst questionnaires and surveys	3
14.	FAF judging on corporate communications	3
15.	Hired outside counsel	2
16.	Have installed stock purchase plans	2
17.	Hired full-time or additional staff personnel	2
18.	Increase quality of publications	2
19.	Toll-free inquiry number	2
20.	Strive for publicity in news media	1
21.	Opinion of peers	1
22.	Maintain mailing lists	1
23.	Corporate contact is VP and member of Executive Committee	1
24.	Have comprehensive investors' kit	1
25.	Company has "open door" policy	1
		208

IR I-6: Is the market performance of your stock important to your company as a corporate objective?

CFA I-8: Should the market performance of the stocks you follow be important to the investor relations efforts of the companies?

		1 No Importance	2 Average Importance	3 Great Importance	Totals
NIRI	Frequency Per Cent	2 1.09	98 53.26	84 46.65	184
CFA	Frequency Per Cent	26 17.69	83 56.45	38 25.85	147
TOTALS	Frequency Per Cent	28 8.46	181 54.68	122 36.86	331

Chi-Square = 35.466   DF = 2   Prob = 0.001

This was a very significant question in the way the respondents answered. Only 25 per cent of the CFAs responded that stock market performance should be of great importance to the companies, while almost half (46 per cent) of the NIRI felt that stock prices is an important corporate objective. Likewise, only 2 (or 1 per cent) NIRI specialists did not believe that stock price should be an objective, while 26 (or 18 per cent of the CFAs believed that stock price should be of "No Importance" to the company as a corporate objective. This leads one to believe that the CFAs do not see market price as a determinant of fundamental value; while the NIRI specialist believes the stock price is of *great* importance.

IR I-7:   In viewing the performance of your company's stock in the marketplace,
how would you rate it?

NIRI		Substan. Under- valued	Moder. Under- valued	Fully Priced	Moder. Over- valued	Substan. Over- valued	Total
Currently	Frequency	21	131	27	4	1	184
	Per Cent	11.413	71.196	14.674	2.174	0.543	100.00
Past 12	Frequency	41	116	24	4	-0-	185
Months	Per Cent	22.162	67.703	12.973	2.162	-0-	100.00
Past 5	Frequency	68	69	35	7	3	182
Years	Per Cent	37.363	37.913	19.231	3.846	1.648	100.00

For the time periods postulated, the investor relations specialists indicate very substantial agreement that their corporations' stocks are "undervalued": (1) currently undervalued (83 per cent); (2) past 12 months (85 per cent); (3) past 5 years (75 per cent). The great majority attribute "moderate" under-valuation to their stocks currently (71 per cent) and to the past 12 months (62 per cent); but they are about equally divided on "moderate" (28 per cent) versus "substantial" (37 per cent) undervaluation for the past 5 years. (An insignificant portion surveyed see their stocks as "overvalued": less than 6 per cent in any time period). This survey result of general undervaluation is significant. It calls attention to the fact that, while most investor relations specialists assert they do a good job in achieving their investor relations objectives (74 per cent) (IR I-2) and are reasonably active in this respect (75 per cent) (IR I-3), they have obviously failed in terms of bringing their corporations' stocks to the status of "full valuation" as a corporate objective. This survey result also clearly indicates an apparent reason they would reject the efficient markets hypothesis of modern investment theory which suggests that common stocks in the capital market are correctly ("fully") priced.

IR I-3, 7:	Correlation between Question 3 and Question 7		
	Question 3		
Question 7A	0.13223	–	Correlation
	0.0752	–	Probability
	182	–	Total observations
Question 7B	0.11535	–	Correlation
	0.1200	–	Probability
	183	–	Total observations
Question 7C	0.06725	–	Correlation
	0.3697	–	Probability
	180	–	Total observations

The possibility of correlation between the level of program activity (Question 3) and the perceived performance of the company's stock (Question 7) was investigated. The resulting correlation coefficients were not significant at the .05 level. Thus, the null hypothesis of no correlation between program activity and stock performance—currently, during the past 12 months and during the past 5 years—could not be rejected.

IR I-8:   Overall, do you believe your investor relations program has had an impact on the market price of your company's stock?

CFA I-9:   Overall, do you believe that investor relations programs of the companies you follow have had an impact on their market price?

		1 *Unfavorable* *Impact*	*2* *No* *Impact*	*3* *Favorable* *Impact*	*4* *Some* *Impact*	*Totals*
NIRI	Frequency	1	30	146	3	180
	Per Cent	.56	16.67	81.11	1.67	
CFA	Frequency	–	45	88	14	147
	Per Cent		30.61	59.86	9.52	
TOTALS	Frequency	1	75	234	17	327
	Per Cent	.31	22.94	71.56	5.20	

Chi-Square = 22.391   DF = 3   Prob. = 0.0001

The chi-square test of significance had a probability of 0.0001, with 3 degrees of freedom, showing that the NIRIs and CFAs marked this question significantly differently. On the Hi-Lo scale, the probability was .0043, which is still very significant, although there was only 1 degree of freedom. In general, the NIRI members tended to mark much higher than the CFAs, with NIRI members marking Cell 3 (Favorable Impact) 81 per cent of the time. An additional category for "Some Impact" was added because of the number of questionnaires (17) which had some type of notation written in. These 2 categories (Cells 3 and 4) accounted for 83 per cent of total investor relations specialists anwering the question. This is contrasted to 70 per cent of the CFAs who answered either Cell 3 or 4. Thirty-one per cent of the CFAs answered that the investor relations programs had no impact on the market price of the stock. While there were no CFAs who felt that an investor relations program had an unfavorable impact on the market price, as did one NIRI respondent, the CFAs, as a group, did tend to see the investor relations activity as being separate from the market performance of the stock.

IR I-9: In terms of your investor relations effort, what do you do, if anything, to influence the price of your company's stock?

		No.
1.	Honest, complete, effective, timely disclosure	41
2.	Active communication with investment community	32
3.	Nothing (don't hype stock)	23
4.	Ongoing program through good and bad, credibility	16
5.	Increased awareness of company	13
6.	Full and open communications	8
7.	Increase investor loyalty	4
8.	Educate analysts to economic factors affecting company	3
9.	Provide access to management	3
10.	Not proper goal	2
11.	Key on areas of positive exposure	2
12.	Effective communication of strategies	2
13.	Encourage participation in dividend reinvestment	2
14.	Produce earnings growth and increase dividend rate	2
15.	Let market set price	1
16.	Monitor investment opinion for lack of perspective	1
17.	Mitigate uncertainty	1
18.	Encourage employee purchase of stock	1
19.	Pay yearly stock dividends	1
		158

CFA I-10:   In terms of their corporate investor relations efforts, what should these
companies do, if anything, to influence the performance of their stock?

		No.
1.	Nothing	25
2.	Disclose valid information to allow fair valuation	25
3.	Simply relay information	18
4.	Disclose adverse as well as favorable developments, explain inconsistencies of results—improving credibility	16
5.	Just be honest	9
6.	Meetings with analysts	9
7.	Financial community exposure	9
8.	Keep lines of communications open	8
9.	Let results, market fix stock price, do not try to "influence"	7
10.	Access to operating management for analysts	5
11.	Presentations to make company more understandable	5
12.	"Grow"	5
13.	Underscore all positives	4
14.	Increase dividends	2
15.	Do NOT promote stock	2
16.	Prevent surprises	2
17.	Buy their own stock	1
18.	Encourage holders to retain holdings	1
19.	Be helpful, not pushy	1
20.	State dividend policy	1
21.	Make forecasts	1
		156

CFA I-II: Overall, do you believe that investor relations programs have had an impact on the market price of a company's stock?

		1 Unfavorable Impact	2 No Impact	3 Some Impact	4 Favorable Impact	Total
CFA	Frequency	-0-	25	103	20	148
	Per Cent		16.89	69.60	13.21	

This question was asked only of the CFAs. The questionnaire had only three responses listed, but because of the number of written-in responses, "Some Impact" was added to denote "some impact." This is where the majority (70 per cent) of answers were marked. It is also interesting that no one felt the investor relations program had an unfavorable impact—generally, the impact, even if slight, was favorable.

IR I-10:   Does your firm have formal, written policies for investor relations?

		Yes	No	Total
NIRI	Frequency	69	116	185
	Per Cent	32.297	62.703	100.00

Only approximately one-third of companies sampled had formal, written policies concerning their investor relations activities. It is at least interesting to note that the SEC (based on previous court cases) is in favor of companies having formal written investor relations policies, although it has not become an SEC requirement.

PART II

IR II-1, 2:   How many security analysts follow your company on both a regular and
          irregular basis?

	0-10	11-20	21-30	31-40	41-50	51-100	100+	Total
Regular	67	33	23	9	18	21	9	180
Irregular	27	40	22	9	18	24	29	169
Total	94	73	45	18	36	45	38	369

The range for analysts following the companies who employed NIRI specialists was from 0-300 analysts. Thirteen reported that they have 10 analysts who follow them on a regular basis, and 14 companies reported that they have 25 analysts following them on a regular basis. Only one company reported that they have 30 analysts following on a regular basis, and 3 companies reported no regular analyst following at all.

On an irregular basis, the companies reported a wider range, from 0-600. Two NIRI members reported that no analysts follow their company on this type of irregular basis, and 1 company each reported 400 analysts, 500 analysts, and 600 analysts who follow irregular. Most companies surveyed appear to have approximately 50 analysts who follow them on an irregular basis (16 companies). Thirteen companies reported that they have 20 analysts following them on this less frequent basis.

IR II-3A: How well do security analysts who follow your company on a regular basis understand the nature of your business?

CFA II-2A: How well do the companies you follow on a regular basis supply you information that allows you to understand the nature of their business?

		1 Very Poorly	2 Below Average	3 Average	4 Above Average	5 Very Well	Totals
NIRI	Frequency Per Cent	1 .56	6 3.33	31 17.22	89 49.44	53 29.44	180
CFA	Frequency Per Cent	— 	6 4.08	31 21.09	80 54.42	30 20.41	147
TOTALS	Frequency Per Cent	1 .31	12 3.67	62 18.96	169 51.68	83 25.38	327

Chi-Square = 4.569   DF = 4   Prob. .3344

Both groups answered this question almost the same; therefore the chi-square value, with 4 degrees of freedom, indicates no significant difference. Both groups marked Cell 4 (Above Average) approximately 50 per cent of the time. On the Hi-Lo scale, no significance was shown between the groups, since 96 per cent of both groups fell in the Hi category. Overall, companies are perceived by analysts as doing a good job in providing information on the nature of the business (75 per cent for Cells 4 and 5); and similarly, companies see analysts as doing a good job in understanding the nature of their business (79 per cent).

IR II-3B: How well do the security analysts who follow your company on a *regular* basis understand the operating and financial risk of your business?

		1 Very Poorly	2 Below Average	3 Average	4 Above Average	5 Very Well	Totals
NIRI	Frequency	–	9	43	79	50	181
	Per Cent		4.97	23.76	43.65	27.62	
CFA	Frequency	2	14	46	62	23	147
	Per Cent	1.36	9.52	31.29	42.18	15.65	
TOTALS	Frequency	2	23	89	141	73	328
	Per Cent	.61	7.01	27.13	42.99	22.26	

Chi-Square = 11.827   DF = 4   Prob. = 0.0187

There was a significant difference in the way the groups marked this question. In general, on both the 1-5 scale and the Hi-Lo scale, the NIRI members marked significantly higher than the CFAs. On the Hi-Lo scale, 95 per cent of the NIRI respondents marked Hi, indicating that they felt the analysts following their company did an average or better job of understanding the operating and the financial risks of their company's business. Some 89 per cent of the CFAs felt that the companies did an average or better job of supplying them with information. Visually, the most significant difference between the groups on the 1-5 scale was that 28 per cent of the NIRI group marked Cell 5 (Very Well) and 24 per cent marked "3" (Average) job done by analysts on understanding their company's operating and financial risks. The CFAs marked "Very Well" only 16 per cent of the time, and 31 per cent said companies were doing an average job of supplying them with information about the operating and financial risks of the company. Overall, each group gives the other somewhat lesser marks than scored on the preceding question: NIRI (71%) and CFAs (58%).

IR II-3C: How well do the security analysts who follow your company on a regular
basis estimate your future earnings?

		1 Very Poorly	2 Below Average	3 Average	4 Above Average	5 Very Well	Totals
NIRI	Frequency	–	16	72	60	32	180
	Per Cent		8.89	40.00	33.33	17.78	
CFA	Frequency	7	19	69	44	3	142
	Per Cent	4.93	13.38	48.59	30.99	2.11	
TOTALS	Frequency	7	35	141	104	35	322
	Per Cent	2.17	10.87	43.79	32.30	10.87	

Chi-Square = 29.741   DF = 4   Prob. = 0.0001

   This question showed a significant difference in both the 1-5 scale and the
Hi-Lo analysis. The NIRI group marked significantly higher than the CFAs,
particularly in Cell 5 (Very Well). Almost 18 per cent of the NIRIs feel that
the analysts are able to estimate their future earnings very well; only 2 per cent
of the CFAs feel that the companies give them enough information enabling
them to estimate future corporate earnings very well (Cell 5); almost 5 per cent
of the CFAs marked Cell 1 (Very Poorly) in regard to how well companies
supply this information. The bulk of the CFAs marked Cell 3 (Average) on
how well companies supply the information. Obviously, the 2 groups part
company in terms of their material assessment.

IR II-3D: How well do analysts who follow your company on a *regular* basis estimate the value of your stock?

CFA II-2D: How well do the companies you follow on a regular basis do in supplying you information that allows you to estimate the value of their stock?

		1 Very Poorly	2 Below Average	3 Average	4 Above Average	5 Very Well	Totals
NIRI	Frequency	1	16	93	47	18	175
	Per Cent	.57	9.14	53.14	26.86	10.29	
CFA	Frequency	15	28	67	25	3	138
	Per Cent	10.87	20.29	48.55	18.12	2.17	
TOTALS	Frequency	16	44	160	72	21	313
	Per Cent	5.11	14.06	51.12	23.00	6.71	

Chi-Square = 33.275   DF = 4   Prob. = 0.0001

This question showed a significant difference between the way the 2 groups answered this question, both on the 1-5 scale and the Hi-Lo scale. For example, CFAs rate the company "Lo," with 11 per cent saying that corporation information received to value the stock was Very Poor (Cell 1), while only 2 per cent of the CFAs rated the information received from the companies as "Very Good" (Cell 5). Only 1 corporate investor relations specialist (.6 per cent) rated the analysts following his company as doing a "Very Poor" job in estimating the value of his company's stock. The NIRI group rated the analysts as either "Above Average" (Cell 4) or "Very Good" (Cell 5) approximately 37 per cent of the time, while the analysts rated the companies either "Above Average" or "Very Good" only 20 per cent of the time. Overall, neither group assesses the other with good marks (Cells 4 and 5) in terms of stock valuation.

IR II-2E: How would you rate the candor of the companies you follow on a regular
             basis in communicating and discussing negative developments?

		1 Very Poorly	2 Below Average	3 Average	4 Above Average	5 Very Well	Totals
CFA	Frequency	7	22	50	54	13	146
	Per Cent	4.80	15.07	34.25	36.99	8.90	

This was another question that was asked only of the CFAs. Generally, the
CFAs felt that the companies did either an average or above average (Cell 3 or
Cell 4) job of communicating negative developments. Less than 20 per cent of
the analysts felt that companies do either a very poor or below average job in
this area. This speaks well of the companies, and their investor relations programs, in the area of full disclosure.

IR II-4, 5:   How many analysts who follow your company on a regular basis, do
               either an excellent or very poor job of evaluating your company?

	-0-	1-10	11-20	21-30	31-40	41-50	51-60	Over 60	Total
Excellent	1	131	23	8	4	3	0	1	187
Very Poor	64	83	6	10	0	1	0	3	167
Total	65	214	29	18	4	4	0	4	354

The NIRI members tend to believe that the majority of analysts do an
excellent job of evaluating their company. Twenty-seven NIRI members feel
that 5 analysts do an excellent job of evaluating their company, while 1 NIRI
member does not believe that any analysts evaluate his company well. One NIRI
member believes that as many as 99 analysts do an excellent job of evaluating his
company. Sixteen NIRI members did not answer this question.

On the other hand, the NIRI members feel that almost none of the
analysts following their company on a regular basis does a very poor job of
evaluation. The number of analysts doing a poor job (as rated by the internal

NIRI specialist) ranges from 0-99. Thirty-eight per cent, or 64, analysts said that no analysts did a poor job.

CFA II-3, 4:   How many of the companies you follow on a regular basis have either an excellent or very poor investor relations program?

	-0-	1-10	11-20	21-30	31-40	41-50	51-60	Over 60	Total
Excellent	5	127	10	3	0	0	1	0	151
Very Poor	24	109	8	1	0	0	1	0	142
Total	29	236	18	4	0	0	1	0	293

The range on companies having excellent investor relations was from 0 to 60 in number. Only 1 analyst said that 60 companies had excellent investor relations programs; ignoring this "outlier," the range was from 0 to 30. Five CFAs did not answer this question. Twenty-nine analysts reported that 5 companies they follow on a regular basis have excellent investor relations programs. Since 27 analysts (the mode) reported that they follow 15 companies on a regular basis, it can be indirectly concluded that approximately 33 per cent of these companies have excellent investor relations programs.

Twenty-five CFAs rate two of the companies they follow as having very poor investor relations programs. The number of companies with poor investor relations programs (as rated by the CFAs) range from 0 to 25. There were several comments indicating that unless the company had a fairly good investor relations program, the analyst would never follow the company in the first place. However, since analysts do tend to follow companies on a regular basis whom they say have poor investor relations programs, this does not appear to be, in fact, a necessary pre-condition for analyst following.

PART III

IR/CFA III-1:   Do you agree or disagree with business segment (line of business) reporting as being helpful in investment decision-making?

		1 Strongly Disagree	2 Moder. Disagree	3 Neutral	4 Moder. Agree	5 Strongly Agree	Totals
NIRI	Frequency	3	13	10	76	82	184
	Per Cent	1.63	7.07	5.43	41.30	44.57	
CFA	Frequency	–	1	4	16	128	149
	Per Cent		.67	2.68	10.74	85.91	
TOTALS	Frequency	3	14	14	92	210	333
	Per Cent	.90	4.20	4.20	27.63	63.06	

Chi-Square = 62.071   DF = 4   Prob. = 0.0001

There was a significant difference, at the .05 level of probability, in the way that the 2 groups felt about line of business reporting. Eighty-five per cent of the CFAs answered that they strongly agreed (Cell 5) with business segment reporting as being helpful in investment decision-making. No analysts marked Cell 1 (Strongly Disagree), and only one analyst marked Cell 2 (Moderately Disagree). The NIRIs did not feel as strongly about this issue; 45 per cent marked Cell 5 (Strongly Agree), and 9 per cent marked either Cell 1 or 2 (Strongly Disagree or Moderately Disagree), about the information being helpful. On the Hi-Lo tables, this same significance was apparent, with CFAs marking higher than the NIRIs.

IR/CFA III-1:   Do you agree or disagree with business segment (line of business) reporting as being helpful in investment decision-making?

		1, 2 Lo	3, 4, 5 High	Totals
NIRI	Frequency	16	168	184
	Per Cent	8.70	91.30	
CFA	Frequency	1	148	149
	Per Cent	.67	99.33	
TOTALS	Frequency	17	316	333
	Per Cent	5.11	94.89	

Chi-Square = 10.943   DF = 1   Prob. = 0.0009

IR/CFA III-2:   Do you agree or disagree with leases capitalized on the balance sheet as being helpful in investment decision-making?

		1 Strongly Disagree	2 Moder. Disagree	3 Neutral	4 Moder. Agree	5 Strongly Agree	Totals
NIRI	Frequency	6	25	74	62	14	181
	Per Cent	3.31	13.81	40.88	34.25	7.73	
CFA	Frequency	6	10	48	57	30	151
	Per Cent	3.97	6.62	31.79	37.75	19.87	
TOTALS	Frequency	12	35	122	119	44	332
	Per Cent	3.61	10.54	36.75	35.84	13.25	

Chi-Square = 15.413   DF = 4   Prob. = 0.0039

On the 1-5 scale, this question showed a significant difference between the NIRI and CFA responses. However, on the Hi-Lo scale, the difference was not significant. Visually testing, the difference was in Cell 5 (Strongly Agree), where the CFAs had a 20 per cent response, and the NIRI group only had an

8 per cent response. The NIRIs marked Cell 2 (Moderately Disagree) 14 per cent, while the CFAs marked Cell 2 only 7 per cent. In general, the CFAs (57 per cent) felt that the lease capitalization issue was more helpful in investment decision-making than did the NIRIs (42 per cent).

IR/CFA III-3:   Do you agree or disagree with footnotes written in "plain English" to assist the small investor in understanding the financial statements as being helpful in investment decision-making?

		1 Strongly Disagree	2 Moder. Disagree	3 Neutral	4 Moder. Agree	5 Strongly Agree	Totals
NIRI	Frequency	2	8	39	66	72	187
	Per Cent	1.07	4.28	20.86	35.29	38.50	
CFA	Frequency	3	6	35	53	54	151
	Per Cent	1.99	3.97	23.18	35.10	35.76	
TOTALS	Frequency	5	14	74	119	126	338
	Per Cent	1.48	4.14	21.89	35.21	37.28	

Chi-Square = 0.869   DF = 4   Prob. = 0.9290

Since both groups would like to see footnotes written in plain English, there was no significant difference in the way that the 2 groups responded. Both groups marked either Cell 4 or 5 over 70 per cent of the time.

However, it is interesting to note that this is one area (footnotes) over which neither the investor relations specialist nor the security analyst is directly involved—this is the function of the corporate accounts and external auditor.

IR/CFA III-4:   Do you agree or disagree with auditor involvement (participation) in quarterly reports as being helpful in investment decision-making?

		1 Strongly Disagree	2 Moder. Disagree	3 Neutral	4 Moder. Agree	5 Strongly Agree	Totals
NIRI	Frequency	30	39	70	35	13	187
	Per Cent	16.04	20.86	37.43	18.74	6.95	
CFA	Frequency	9	19	62	41	19	150
	Per Cent	6.00	12.67	41.33	27.33	12.67	
TOTALS	Frequency	39	58	132	76	32	337
	Per Cent	11.57	17.21	39.17	22.55	9.50	

Chi-Square = 16.424   DF = 4   Prob. = 0.0025

The CFAs and NIRIs marked this question significantly differently with the CFAs preferring more involvement by the auditors than the NIRI (40 per cent versus 25 per cent). However, this was not considered extremely important by either group. Almost 40 per cent of both groups had no feeling one way or the other (marked Cell 3—Neutral) on the question. Another 40 per cent of the CFAs marked either Cell 4 or 5 (Moderately or Strongly Agree), while only 25 per cent of the NIRI marked these cells.

IR/CFA III-5: Do you agree or disagree with explicit disclosure of auditors' fees as being helpful in investment decision-making?

		1 Strongly Disagree	2 Moder. Disagree	3 Neutral	4 Moder. Agree	5 Strongly Agree	Totals
NIRI	Frequency	45	43	76	12	11	187
	Per Cent	24.06	22.99	40.64	6.42	5.88	
CFA	Frequency	22	41	69	8	9	149
	Per Cent	14.77	27.52	46.31	5.37	6.04	
TOTALS	Frequency	67	84	145	20	20	336
		19.94	25.00	43.15	5.95	5.95	

Chi-Square = 5.048   DF = 4   Prob. = 0.2824

The results of this question showed no significant difference between the way that the 2 groups marked. Both NIRIs and CFAs answered the question uniformly across all 5 levels. In this question, 40 per cent of both groups marked Cell 3 (Neutral), while the other approximately 40 per cent marked Cell 1 or 2 (Strongly or Moderately Disagree). It would appear that neither group feels that explicit disclosure of auditors' fees is helpful in investment decision-making.

IR/CFA III-6:   Do you agree or disagree that explicit supplementary disclosure of
investor relations costs for the past year is helpful in investment decision-making?

		1 Strongly Disagree	2 Moder. Disagree	3 Neutral	4 Moder. Agree	5 Strongly Agree	Totals
NIRI	Frequency	69	42	70	8	2	187
	Per Cent	34.76	22.46	37.43	4.28	1.07	
CFA	Frequency	27	39	60	16	6	148
	Per Cent	18.24	26.35	40.54	10.81	4.05	
TOTALS	Frequency	94	81	130	24	8	335
	Per Cent	27.46	24.18	38.81	7.16	2.39	

Chi-Square = 16.932   DF = 4   Prob. = 0.0020

This question appears to strike close to the hearts of the NIRI group,
since only approximately 5 per cent thought this would be a helpful investment
decision-making tool. Only 15 per cent of the CFAs felt it would be a helpful
figure. Although there was a significant difference in the way the groups marked
this question, both tended to feel that it was obviously not important to investment decision-making. The NIRIs appeared very reluctant to disclose their
internal investor relations costs; 57 per cent marked Cell 1 or 2 (Strongly or
Moderately Disagree).

IR/CFA III-7: Do you agree or disagree with replacement cost information as being helpful in investment decision-making?

		1 Strongly Disagree	2 Moder. Disagree	3 Neutral	4 Moder. Agree	5 Strongly Agree	Totals
NIRI	Frequency	48	39	42	49	7	185
	Per Cent	25.95	21.08	22.70	26.49	3.78	
CFA	Frequency	9	25	48	46	19	147
	Per Cent	6.12	17.01	32.65	31.29	12.93	
TOTALS	Frequency	57	64	90	95	26	332
	Per Cent	17.17	19.28	27.11	28.61	7.83	

Chi-Square = 31.848   DF = 4   Prob. = 0.0001

This question appeared to be a very important one. There was a very significant difference in the way that the CFAs and NIRIs responded. The significance level was 0.0001 for both the 1-5 scale and the Hi-Lo scale. However, the differences showed up most dramatically in the Hi-Lo chart. The CFAs feel very strongly that replacement cost information is helpful. The NIRIs divided almost evenly, with 53 per cent marking Cell 3, 4, or 5, and 47 per cent marking Cell 1 or 2. This compares with the CFAs who had 76 per cent marking the Hi scale (3, 4, and 5), and only 23 per cent rating replacement cost information as Lo (1 or 2) in being helpful in making investment decisions. Even more interesting is that 13 per cent of the CFAs marked Cell 5 (Strongly Agree) stating that they consider replacement cost information as being very helpful in making investment decisions, but only 4 per cent of NIRI members marked Cell 5. Also, 36 per cent of NIRIs marked Cell 1 (Strongly Disagree), while only 6 per cent of CFAs marked the same cell.

This leads one to the view that corporations appear to have taken—that replacement cost accounting generally is worthless and meaningless, but still required by the SEC. The analysts, however, appear to want the information, regardless of its allegedly low quality.

IR/CFA III-7:   Do you agree or disagree with replacement cost information as being helpful in investment decision-making.

		1, 2 Lo	3, 4, 5 High	Totals
NIRI	Frequency Per Cent	87 47.03	98 52.97	185
CFA	Frequency Per Cent	34 23.13	113 76.87	147
TOTALS	Frequency Per Cent	211 63.55	121 36.45	332

Chi-Square = 20.196   DF = 1   Prob. = 0.0001

IR/CFA III-8:   Do you agree or disagree with dividend policy, stated in terms of payout ratio as being helpful in investment decision-making?

		1 Strongly Disagree	2 Moder. Disagree	3 Neutral	4 Moder. Agree	5 Strongly Agree	Totals
NIRI	Frequency Per Cent	20 10.75	23 12.37	39 20.97	62 33.33	42 22.58	186
CFA	Frequency Per Cent	3 2.00	9 6.00	22 14.67	70 46.67	46 30.67	150
TOTALS	Frequency Per Cent	23 6.85	32 9.52	61 18.51	132 39.29	88 26.19	336

Chi-Square = 20.472   DF = 4   Prob. = 0.0004

This question shows a significant difference between the CFAs and NIRIs at the .05 level. CFAs felt the dividend policy information was more important for investment decision-making than did the NIRI group; 77 per cent of CFAs ranked this information either Cell 4 or 5 (Moderately or Strongly Agree), while only 56 per cent of NIRIs marked it in these columns. On the other hand,

23 per cent of the NIRIs marked this information as being unimportant (Cell 1 or 2), compared with 8 per cent of CFAs marking it the same way. The Hi-Lo chart indicates this same difference in markings.

IR/CFA III-8:   Do you agree or disagree with dividend policy stated in terms of payout ratio as being helpful in investment decision-making?

		1, 2 Lo	3, 4, 5 High	Totals
NIRI	Frequency	43	143	186
	Per Cent	23.12	76.88	
CFA	Frequency	12	138	150
	Per Cent	8.00	92.00	
TOTALS	Frequency	55	281	336
	Per Cent	16.37	83.63	

Chi-Square = 13.864   DF = 1   Prob. = 0.0002

IR/CFA III-9:   Do you agree or disagree with capital expenditures planned for the next 12 months as being helpful in investment decision-making?

		1 Strongly Disagree	2 Moder. Disagree	3 Neutral	4 Moder. Agree	5 Strongly Agree	Totals
NIRI	Frequency	4	10	21	77	70	182
	Per Cent	2.20	5.49	11.54	42.31	38.46	
CFA	Frequency	–	2	4	44	99	149
	Per Cent		1.34	2.68	29.53	66.44	
TOTALS	Frequency	4	12	25	121	169	331
	Per Cent	1.21	3.63	7.55	36.56	51.06	

Chi-Square = 31.897   DF = 4   Prob. = 0.0001

This question also indicates a difference in CFAs and the NIRIs, as to the desirability of forward-looking information for investment decision-making. The CFAs marked Cells 4 and 5 (Moderately Agree and Strongly Agree) 96 per cent of the time—obviously considering capital expenditures planned as one of the most important pieces of information they can be given. NIRI representatives agreed with this information as being important (Cell 4 or 5) 81 per cent of the time. Interestingly, no CFAs even marked Cell 1 (Strongly Disagree), and only 8 per cent of the NIRIs marked either Cell 1 or 2. While the differences were extremely significant on the 1-5 scale, they were not quite as significant (0.007) on the Hi-Lo scale.

IR/CFA III-9:   Do you agree or disagree with capital expenditures planned for the next 12 months as being helpful in investment decision-making?

		1, 2, Lo	3, 4, 5 High	Totals
NIRI	Frequency	14	168	182
	Per Cent	7.69	92.31	
CFA	Frequency	2	147	149
	Per Cent	1.34	98.66	
TOTALS	Frequency	16	315	331
	Per Cent	4.83	95.17	

Chi-Square = 7.181   DF = 1   Prob. = 0.0074

IR/CFA III-10:   Do you agree or disagree with target debt-equity ratio to be maintained in future years as being helpful in investment decision-making?

		1 Strongly Disagree	2 Moder. Disagree	3 Neutral	4 Moder. Agree	5 Strongly Agree	Totals
NIRI	Frequency	9	23	34	79	39	184
	Per Cent	4.89	12.50	18.48	42.93	21.20	
CFA	Frequency	1	3	18	63	65	150
	Per Cent	.67	2.00	12.00	42.00	43.33	
TOTALS	Frequency	10	26	52	142	104	334
	Per Cent	2.29	7.78	15.57	42.51	31.14	

Chi-Square = 31.880   DF = 4   Prob. = 0.0001

Target debt-equity ratios show a significant difference in both the 1-5 scale and the Hi-Lo scale, at the 0.05 level. (Both groups agree that it is important: NIRIs 64 per cent and CFAs 85 per cent). The major difference, as determined by a visual inspection of the data, appears to be in Cell 1 (Strongly Disagree), where less than 1 per cent of CFAs think the information is unimportant for investment decision-making, while 5 per cent of the NIRIs strongly disagree with the information as being useful. Also, 43 per cent of CFAs feel that the information is very important (Cell 5), while only 21 per cent of the NIRI consider the information very important. Both CFAs and NIRIs marked Cell 4 (Moderately Agree) approximately 42 per cent of the time. Franco Modigliani and Merton H. Miller[4] in the theoretical literature made a major issue out of this point, believing that this is how companies operate.

IR/CFA III-10:   Do you agree or disagree with target debt-equity ratio to be maintained in future years as being helpful in investment decision-making?

		1, 2 Lo	3, 4, 5 High	Totals
NIRI	Frequency	32	152	184
	Per Cent	17.39	82.61	
CFA	Frequency	4	146	150
	Per Cent	2.67	97.33	
TOTALS	Frequency	36	298	334
	Per Cent	10.78	89.22	

Chi-Square = 18.631   DF = 1   Prob. = 0.0001

IR/CFA III-11:   Do you agree or disagree with a management forecast of sales (point or range) for the next 12 months as being important in investment decision-making?

		1 Strongly Disagree	2 Moder. Disagree	3 Neutral	4 Moder. Agree	5 Strongly Agree	Totals
NIRI	Frequency	36	38	22	67	22	185
	Per Cent	19.46	20.54	11.89	36.22	11.89	
CFA	Frequency	8	11	32	56	43	150
	Per Cent	5.33	7.33	21.33	37.33	28.67	
TOTALS	Frequency	44	49	54	123	65	335
	Per Cent	13.13	14.63	16.12	36.72	19.40	

Chi-Square = 39.086   DF = 4   Prob. = 0.0001

Forecasting sales, while marked significantly differently by the NIRIs and CFAs, is not marked as being as important as other information (i.e., target debt-equity ratio) by either group. CFAs marked this as an important investment decision-making tool (Cell 4 or 5) 66 per cent of the time, and the NIRIs marked the same cells only 48 per cent of the time. The NIRIs marked Cell 1 or 2 (Strongly Disagree or Moderately Disagree) 40 per cent of the time. The CFAs, on this same scale, marked Cell 1 or 2 only 13 per cent of the time. Obviously, the NIRI members appear very reluctant to give this information, while the CFAs consider other information more helpful. This goes to the heart of "soft" information disclosure, which is a highly controversial subject in the theoretical literature.

IR/CFA III-11: Do you agree or disagree with a management forecast of sales (point or range) for the next 12 months as being helpful in investment decision-making?

		1, 2 Lo	3, 4, 5 High	Totals
NIRI	Frequency	74	111	185
	Per Cent	40.00	60.00	
CFA	Frequency	19	131	150
	Per Cent	12.67	87.33	
TOTALS	Frequency	93	242	335
	Per Cent	27.76	72.24	

Chi-Square = 30.860   DF = 1   Prob. = 0.0001

IR/CFA III-12:   Do you agree or disagree with a management forecast of earnings (point or range) for the next 12 months as being helpful in investment decision-making?

		1 Strongly Disagree	2 Moder. Disagree	3 Neutral	4 Moder. Agree	5 Strongly Agree	Totals
NIRI	Frequency	63	31	20	56	17	187
	Per Cent	33.69	16.58	10.70	29.95	9.09	
CFA	Frequency	16	11	35	56	31	149
	Per Cent	10.74	7.38	23.49	37.58	20.81	
TOTALS	Frequency	79	42	55	112	48	336
	Per Cent	23.51	12.50	16.37	33.33	14.29	

Chi-Square = 41.898   DF = 4   Prob. = 0.0001

Forecasting earnings (marked as significantly different) appears to generate considerable disfavor and disapproval among NIRI members. Over 50 per cent marked Cell 1 or 2 (Strongly Disagree or Moderately Disagree), while on 18 per cent of the CFAs marked the same cells. The NIRIs also feel somewhat more strongly about their not revealing earnings than revealing sales. The CFAs still favor the release of future earnings projections, but also not as strongly as releasing sales forecasts. Interestingly, only 20 per cent of CFAs marked Cell 5 (Strongly Agree) that forecast of earnings is helpful in investment decision-making, while 9 per cent of the NIRI members marked this cell. It would appear that the NIRI members are more anxious *not* to give the information than the CFAs are to get it. This same significance appears in the Hi-Lo chart.

IR/CFA III-12:   Do you agree or disagree with a management forecast of earnings (point or range) for the next 12 months as being helpful in investment decision-making?

		1, 2 Lo	3, 4, 5 High	Totals
NIRI	Frequency	94	93	187
	Per Cent	50.27	49.73	
CFA	Frequency	27	122	139
	Per Cent	18.12	81.88	
TOTALS	Frequency	121	215	336
	Per Cent	36.01	63.99	

Chi-Square = 37.189   DF = 1   Prob. = 0.0001

IR/CFA III-13:   Do you agree or disagree with management forecast of earnings per share (point or range) for the next 12 months as being important in investment decision-making?

		1 Strongly Disagree	2 Moder Disagree	3 Neutral	4 Moder. Agree	5 Strongly Agree	Totals
NIRI	Frequency	62	33	21	53	16	185
	Per Cent	33.51	17.84	11.35	28.65	8.65	
CFA	Frequency	19	11	35	52	30	147
	Per Cent	12.93	7.48	23.81	35.37	20.41	
TOTALS	Frequency	81	44	56	105	46	332
	Per Cent	24.40	13.25	16.87	31.63	13.86	

Chi-Square = 37.743   DF = 4   Prob. = 0.0001

This question was marked almost exactly as the previous question concerning forecast of aggregate earnings. Also, the same level of significance showed on the Hi-Lo chart. While 56 per cent of the CFAs felt that this information would be helpful in making investment decisions (Cell 4 or 5), only

37 per cent of the NIRIs marked it the same way. Cell 1 or 2 (Strongly Disagree or Moderately Disagree) was marked by the NIRIs 51 per cent of the time, and the CFAs marked it 20 per cent.

IR/CFA III-13:   Do you agree or disagree with management forecast of earnings per share (point or range) for the next 12 months as being important in investment decision-making?

		1, 2 Lo	3, 4, 5 High	Totals
NIRI	Frequency	95	90	185
	Per Cent	51.35	48.65	
CFA	Frequency	30	117	147
	Per Cent	20.41	79.59	
TOTALS	Frequency	125	207	332
	Per Cent	37.65	62.35	

Chi-Square = 33.410   DF = 1   Prob. = 0.0001

IR/CFA III-1-13:   *Grouped Analysis*

The individual information questions were grouped into blocks representing a more composite picture of the information discerned to be pertinent to the NIRIs and CFAs. The direction of their preferences overall could indicate whether historical (hard) or forward-looking (soft) information was deemed to be of more importance. Multi-way contingency tables were used in this analysis, and are available on request.

The first six questions within Part III (Information Section) dealt with historical information. A multi-way contingency table was used to determine whether one group placed more emphasis on the necessity of these questions than the other. The resulting significance level of 0.0520 indicated that the hypothesis of no difference could not be rejected. The CFAs tended to be more in agreement with the necessity of inclusion of hard information; however, this could be seen only as a trend, since the significance level was greater than the accepted .05 level of significance.

Questions 7 through 10 of Part III obtained results similar to Questions 1 through 6. These questions were considered soft (forward-looking) in context, and although the CFAs responded to the individual areas of information with significantly more approval than did the NIRIs, there was not enough difference to be considered statistically significant at the .05 level. The analyses were performed, including the neutral attitude (Cell 3) with the low responses, as well as including it with the high responses. Identical results were obtained under each method.

In general, the CFAs always marked higher than the NIRIs, indicating that CFAs are always interested in obtaining additional information. Interestingly, if the NIRIs have to give additional information, they would prefer to give certain kinds of soft information (debt/equity ratios; capital expenditures) than to furnish specific forecasts of sales, earnings, and earnings per share.

The final block of questions in Part III (Questions 11-13) had different results. A forward-looking philosophy was reflected within the context. The CFAs not only responded significantly more strongly concerning the importance of each question, they also were significantly different from the NIRIs over the entire area; they agree that this type of information (forecast of sales, earnings, and earnings per share) is helpful. Therefore, the hypothesis of no difference between the NIRIs and CFAs with respect to forward-oriented information is rejected.

In summary of Questions 1 through 13 in Part III, there is no significant difference between the NIRI group and CFAs with respect to the desirability of historical information, although there is a strong trend toward the CFAs preferring this type of information. However, there is a significant difference between the groups on the forward-looking information, with the CFAs wanting this information and the NIRIs' preferring not to give it, or at least thinking it is not helpful to investment decision-making.

IR/CFA III-14:   Do you agree or disagree that more information is now being required of corporations by the SEC than is necessary to ensure efficient capital markets?

		1 Strongly Disagree	2 Moder. Disagree	3 Neutral	4 Moder. Agree	5 Strongly Agree	Totals
NIRI	Frequency	9	25	39	65	47	185
	Per Cent	4.86	13.51	21.08	35.14	25.41	
CFA	Frequency	23	39	36	24	24	146
	Per Cent	15.75	26.71	24.66	16.44	16.44	
TOTALS	Frequency	32	64	75	89	71	331
	Per Cent	9.67	19.34	22.66	26.89	21.45	

Chi-Square = 31.488   DF = 4   Prob. = 0.0001

As one would expect, the NIRI group answered this question significantly differently from the CFAs on the amount of information being required by the SEC at the present time. The NIRIs (who represent the corporate view) believe that the SEC requires too much information (60 per cent). This information becomes a cost that is borne largely by the corporation. The CFAs, by 42 per cent, however, who are the users of this information, want more information (Cells 1 and 2). It appears to be a relatively clear indication that if the user of information has his way, the SEC will continue the pressure for more and more corporate disclosure.

IF/CFA III-14:   Do you agree or disagree that more information is now being required
of corporations by the SEC than is necessary to ensure efficient capital markets?

		1, 2 Lo	3, 4, 5 High	Totals
NIRI	Frequency	34	151	185
	Per Cent	18.38	81.62	
CFA	Frequency	62	84	146
	Per Cent	42.47	57.53	
TOTALS	Frequency	96	235	331
	Per Cent	29.00	71.00	

Chi-Square = 22.993   DF = 1   Prob. = 0.0001

IR III-15:   Please list any information (either "hard" or "soft," historical or forward-looking) that you believe corporations should furnish, but are not now disclosing, that would be helpful in investment decision-making.

		No.
1.	Business segment reporting	5
2.	Information on strategy, long-term goals and objectives	5
3.	Nothing more needed	5
4.	Forecasts	4
5.	Cost of, effect of, government compliance	3
6.	Market share data	3
7.	ROE and ROI goals	3
8.	Managment succession and development	2
9.	Management experience and backgrounds	2
10.	Capital expenditure allocations	2
11.	Quality of markets	2
12.	Institutional holdings	2
13.	Currency translation effects	2
14.	Foreign assets	1
15.	*Full* disclosure	1
16.	True "float" of stock	1
17.	Quality of management	1
18.	Sales backlog data	1
19.	Statement of dividend policy	1
20.	Cash flow analysis	1
21.	"Current value" reporting	1
22.	Eliminate FASB 8	1
23.	R&D funding	1
24.	Pension costs and funding	1
25.	Rolling 12-months earnings	1

52

CFA III-15: Please list any information (either "hard" or "soft," historical or forward-looking) that you believe corporations should furnish, but are not now disclosing, that would be helpful in decision-making.

		No.
1.	Segment reporting (impact on bottom line)—also product line	17
2.	Industry trends	6
3.	Market share data	4
4.	Evaluation of competitive position	4
5.	Competitive impact of major developments (bottom line effect also)	4
6.	*All* currency effects	3
7.	Better discourse on problem areas	3
8.	Long-term corporate strategy (goals, objectives)	4
9.	Pricing policy	3
10.	Pension costs	2
11.	Market trends	2
12.	Inputs used in making company forecasts	2
13.	Forecasts of sales, earnings, margins	2
14.	R&D allocations	2
15.	Gross margins	1
16.	Wages as per cent of sales	1
17.	Inventory age	1
18.	Depreciation (methods, basis)	1
19.	Real growth of sales	1
20.	Financing plans	1
21.	Estimate of current quarterly earnings	1
22.	Capital expenditure outlook	1
23.	Backlog data	1
24.	Effects of leverage	1
25.	Inventory profits	1
26.	Unit volumes (same store's sales gains)	1
27.	Directors, management, employees stock holdings	1
28.	Unit cost trends (inventory)	1
		72

Other Comments:
1. "It's all there (if you know how to read it)."
2. "Why should company provide 'forward looking' information to competitors?"
3. "Replacement cost accounting not in best interest of shareholders."
4. "FASB 8 all screwed up."

PART IV

IR/CFA IV-1:   Do you agree or disagree with the academic view that security price
changes are random and unpredictable (i.e., they form a "random walk")?

---

		1 *Strongly* *Disagree*	2 *Moder.* *Disagree*	3 *Neutral*	4 *Moder.* *Agree*	5 *Strongly* *Agree*	*Totals*
NIRI	Frequency	38	74	21	49	3	185
	Per Cent	20.54	40.00	11.35	26.49	1.62	
CFA	Frequency	54	51	12	24	7	148
	Per Cent	36.49	34.46	8.11	16.22	4.73	
TOTALS	Frequency	92	125	33	73	10	333
	Per Cent	27.63	37.54	9.91	21.92	3.00	

Chi-Square = 15.714   DF = 4   Prob. = 0.0034

Both NIRIs and CFAs disagree with this statement, but more CFAs (70 per cent) marked Cells 1 and 2 (Strongly Disagree or Moderately Disagree) than did the NIRIs (60 per cent). This is a rather surprising statistic, since the CFAs have had more exposure to fundamental analysis and to modern investment theory, which denies any useful role to technical analysis.

While there is a significant difference in the way the NIRIs and CFAs marked the 1-5 scale (difference of 0.0034 at the .05 level), there is no significant difference on the Hi-Lo Scale. In this scale, both CFAs and NIRI disagree with the theory of random walk, i.e., that price changes are random and unpredictable.

IR/CFA IV-1:   Do you agree or disagree with the academic view that security price changes are random and unpredictable (i.e., they form a "random walk")?

		1, 2 Lo	3, 4, 5 High	Totals
NIRI	Frequency Per Cent	112 60.54	72 39.46	185
CFA	Frequency Per Cent	105 70.95	43 29.05	148
TOTALS	Frequency Per Cent	217 65.17	116 34.83	333

Chi-Square = 3.922   DF = 1   Prob. = 0.0477

IR/CFA IV-2:   Do you agree or disagree with the academic view that knowledge of historical patterns of stock prices (work of the "chartists") does not aid investors in attaining improved investment performance?

		1 Strongly Disagree	2 Moder. Disagree	3 Neutral	4 Moder. Agree	5 Strongly Agree	Totals
NIRI	Frequency Per Cent	12 6.42	72 38.50	35 18.72	55 29.41	13 6.95	187
CFA	Frequency Per Cent	19 12.93	63 42.86	24 16.33	27 18.37	14 9.52	147
TOTALS	Frequency Per Cent	31 9.28	135 40.42	59 17.66	82 24.55	27 8.08	334

Chi-Square = 9.171   DF = 4   Prob. = 0.0570

This question does not show a significant difference in the way that the CFAs and the NIRIs marked. However, more than the chi-square difference, the way the groups marked the cells is interesting and important. The

CFAs marked Cells 1 and 2 (Strongly Disagree or Moderately Disagree) approximately 55 per cent of the time, while the NIRIs marked the same cells approximaely 45 per cent of the time. This indicates that both groups reject the theory that the work of chartists is useless; and corroborates the same view as expounded in the previous question. Again, this is a surprising view, since the CFAs have had substantial training in fundamental analysis and in modern investment theory, which is a direct challenge to technical analysis.

IR/CFA IV-3:   Do you agree or disagree with the academic view that publicly available information on securities is quickly discounted by the securities market?

		1 Strongly Disagree	2 Moder. Disagree	3 Neutral	4 Moder. Agree	5 Strongly Agree	Totals
NIRI	Frequency	2	36	17	108	24	187
	Per Cent	1.07	19.25	9.09	57.75	12.83	
CFA	Frequency	6	31	15	70	24	146
	Per Cent	4.11	21.23	10.27	47.95	16.44	
TOTALS	Frequency	8	67	32	178	48	333
	Per Cent	2.40	20.12	9.61	53.45	14.41	

Chi-Square = 5.648   DF = 4   Prob. = 0.2270

There is no significant difference in the way that the CFAs and NIRIs answered this question. Both groups believe that information is discounted quickly by the securities market. Seventy per cent of the NIRIs believe that the information they generate is quickly discounted by the market, and the CFAs agree by 64 per cent. Interestingly, approximately 20 per cent of both groups believe that the market is slow in assimilating the information. This question generally affirms the random walk theory, and efficiency of the securities markets. This is a contradictory response to the previous two questions.

IR/CFA IV-4:   Do you agree or disagree with the academic view that stock prices at any point in time will represent good estimates of intrinsic or fundamental values?

		1 Strongly Disagree	2 Moder. Disagree	3 Neutral	4 Moder. Agree	5 Strongly Agree	Totals
NIRI	Frequency	42	83	16	45	1	187
	Per Cent	22.46	44.39	8.56	24.06	.53	
CFA	Frequency	30	58	14	50	5	147
	Per Cent	20.41	39.46	9.52	27.21	3.40	
TOTALS	Frequency	72	141	30	85	6	334
	Per Cent	21.56	42.22	8.98	25.45	1.80	

Chi-Square = 4.805   DF = 4   Prob. = 0.3079

This question does not show a significant chi-square difference for the two groups. Both groups marked Cell 1 or 2 (Strongly Disagree or Moderately Disagree), indicating that they believe the capital market does a poor job in assessing values, which is another way of stating that stocks are often undervalued or overvalued. This is a denial of the semi-strong and strong forms of the efficient markets hypothesis. Approximately 60 per cent of both groups marked Cell 1 or 2, while only 6 individuals (5 who are CFAs and one who is a member of NIRI) marked Cell 5 (Strongly Agree).

IR/CFA IV-5: Do you agree or disagree with the academic view that a stock split increases the total value of the corporation's shares outstanding?

		1 Strongly Disagree	2 Moder. Disagree	3 Neutral	4 Moder. Agree	5 Strongly Agree	Totals
NIRI	Frequency	12	35	30	12	12	185
	Per Cent	6.49	18.92	16.22	51.89	6.49	
CFA	Frequency	17	40	28	57	6	148
	Per Cent	11.49	27.03	18.92	38.51	4.05	
TOTALS	Frequency	29	75	58	153	18	333
	Per Cent	8.71	22.52	17.42	45.95	5.41	

Chi-Square = 9.208   DF = 4   Prob. = 0.0561

The two groups showed no significant difference in the way that they marked this question. The NIRIs feel positively about this question, with 52 per cent marking Cell 4 (Moderately Agree), while the CFAs are less inclined to this view (39 per cent marking Cell 4). While the two groups disagree mildly, this is understandable: the investor relations specialist wants more stock available for public trading and more active trading in the stock. The CFAs have no similar inducement to believe that a stock split impacts on market value. Eugene F. Fama finds that no effect should take place,[5] apart from any cash dividend effect, as the stock split has been fully discounted by the declaration rate. Theory, therefore, does not uphold the power of a stock split, as implied by the practices of corporations.

IR/CFA IV-5:   Do you agree or disagree with the academic view that apart from any cash dividend effects, a stock split increases the total value of the corporation's shares outstanding because investors are more inclined to purchase lower priced securities?

		1, 2, 3 Lo	4, 5 High	Totals
NIRI	Frequency	77	108	185
	Per Cent	41.622	58.378	
CFA	Frequency	85	63	148
	Per Cent	57.432	42.568	
TOTALS	Frequency	162	171	333
	Per Cent	48.649	51.351	

IR/CFA IV-5:   Do you agree or disagree with the academic view that apart from any cash dividend effects, a stock split increases the total value of the corporation's shares outstanding because investors are more inclined to purchase lower priced securities?

		1, 2 Lo	3, 4, 5 High	Totals
NIRI	Frequency	47	138	185
	Per Cent	25.41	74.59	
CFA	Frequency	57	91	148
	Per Cent	38.51	61.49	
TOTALS	Frequency	104	229	333
	Per Cent	31.23	68.77	

Chi-square = 6.578   DF = 1   Prob. = 0.0103

In this question, the 1-5 scale showed no significant difference between the way that the NIRIs and CFAs marked the scale. However, when the responses were arrayed in a Hi-Lo scale, there was a significant difference.

This question was tested using Lo as 1, 2, 3 and High as 4, 5, which gave a chi-square value of 8.23 and a probability of .004. Then, the question was tested again using Lo values as 1, 2 and Hi as 3, 4, 5; this test gave a chi-square of 6.578 and a probability of .0103. In this particular case, the most conservative way to figure the Hi-Lo was with Lo as 1, 2 and Hi as 3, 4, 5.

The chi-square test over all categories did not reflect a difference large enough to be significant. The distribution was approximate. However, when re-grouped in the foregoing manner, the differences that had been spread out over five categories now became more apparent.

IR/CFA IV-6:   Do you agree or disagree with the academic view that "good news" is disseminated to the market more promptly by corporations than "bad news"?

		1 Strongly Disagree	2 Moder. Disagree	3 Neutral	4 Moder. Agree	5 Strongly Agree	Totals
NIRI	Frequency	20	35	21	86	24	186
	Per Cent	10.75	18.82	11.29	46.24	12.90	
CFA	Frequency	13	18	19	59	38	147
	Per Cent	8.84	12.24	12.93	40.14	25.85	
TOTALS	Frequency	33	53	40	145	62	333
	Per Cent	9.91	15.92	12.01	43.54	18.62	

Chi-Square = 10.807   DF = 4   Prob. = 0.0288

This question was marked differently by the two groups at the .02 level. The major difference is in the way that Cell 5 (Strongly Agree) was marked: NIRI members marked Cell 5 only 13 per cent, while the CFAs marked Cell 5 about 26 per cent, indicating that the CFAs believe that good news often is disseminated more quickly than bad news. This is an understandable break-down: the CFAs are the receivers of the information, and the NIRIs are responsible for disseminating the news, whether good or bad. Indeed, the NIRI has the charge in the NIRI code of ethics of disseminating information promptly. It is interesting to note that even 58 per cent of the NIRIs tend to agree (Cell 4 or 5) that good information is disseminated more quickly than bad news. The significance between the two groups is not discernible when calculated on the Hi-Lo basis.

IR/CFA IV-6: Do you agree or disagree with the academic view that "good news" is disseminated to the market more promptly by corporations than "bad news"?

		1, 2 Lo	3, 4, 5 High	Totals
NIRI	Frequency	55	131	186
	Per Cent	29.57	70.43	
CFA	Frequency	31	116	147
	Per Cent	21.09	78.91	
TOTALS	Frequency	86	247	333
	Per Cent	25.83	74.17	

Chi-Square = 3.083   DF = 1   Prob. = 0.0791

IR/CFA IV-7: Do you agree or disagree with the academic view that most published security analysis is logically incomplete and valueless?

		1 Strongly Disagree	2 Moder. Disagree	3 Neutral	4 Moder. Agree	5 Strongly Agree	Totals
NIRI	Frequency	53	87	27	15	3	185
	Per Cent	28.65	47.03	14.59	8.11	1.62	
CFA	Frequency	43	57	23	19	5	147
	Per Cent	29.25	38.78	15.65	12.93	3.40	
TOTALS	Frequency	96	144	50	34	8	332
	Per Cent	28.92	43.37	15.06	10.24	2.41	

Chi-Square = 4.289   DF = 4   Prob. = 0.3683

This question shows no significant difference between the two groups. Both groups disagree with this statement decisively: CFAs marked Cell 1 or 2 some 68 per cent of the time, while NIRIs marked these cells 75 per cent of the time. The question is formulated via the efficient markets hypothesis as a direct challenge on the value of fundamental analysis, the end product on which both groups' livelihood depends. Less than 10 per cent of the NIRIs and less than 16 per cent of the CFAs agree with this statement.

IR/CFA IV-8:	Do you agree or disagree with the academic view that there are more security analysts than are needed to keep the stock market efficient?					

		1 Strongly Disagree	2 Moder. Disagree	3 Neutral	4 Moder. Agree	5 Strongly Agree	Totals
NIRI	Frequency	52	65	37	26	7	187
	Per Cent	27.81	34.76	19.79	13.90	3.74	
CFA	Frequency	27	38	40	41	2	148
	Per Cent	18.24	25.68	27.03	27.70	1.35	
TOTALS	Frequency	79	103	77	67	9	335
	Per Cent	23.58	30.75	22.99	20.00	2.69	

Chi-Square = 16.931   DF = 4   Prob. = 0.0020

This question was marked significantly differently by the two groups. The chi-square is significant at the 0.002 level. Approximately 62 per cent of the NIRIs and 43 per cent of the CFAs disagree (marked Cell 1 or 2) that there are too many analysts. The results were not surprising for the NIRI, since the more analysts there are, the better covered through analysis the company will be. The surprising result was for the CFAs, since their jobs, and opportunities for promotion, depend on the total population of analysts. One would expect a stronger affirmation for this profession. Less than 4 per cent of the NIRIs and less than 2 per cent of the CFAs agree (Cell 5) with the idea that there are more analysts than necessary to keep the stock market efficient.

IR/CFA IV-8: Do you agree or disagree with the academic view that there are more security analysts than are needed to keep the stock market efficient?

		1, 2, Lo	3, 4, 5 High	Totals
NIRI	Frequency Per Cent	117 62.57	70 37.43	187
CFA	Frequency Per Cent	65 43.92	83 56.08	148
TOTALS	Frequency Per Cent	182 54.33	153 45.67	335

Chi-Square = 11.578   DF = 1   Prob. = 0.0007

IR/CFA IV-9: Do you agree or disagree with the academic view that beta is the single most important measure of a security's risk?

		1 Strongly Disagree	2 Moder. Disagree	3 Neutral	4 Moder. Agree	5 Strongly Agree	Totals
NIRI	Frequency Per Cent	53 28.65	74 40.00	45 24.32	12 6.49	1 0.54	185
CFA	Frequency Per Cent	53 35.81	51 34.46	25 16.89	15 10.14	4 2.70	148
TOTALS	Frequency Per Cent	106 31.83	125 37.54	70 21.02	27 8.11	5 1.50	333

Chi-Square = 8.068   DF = 4   Prob. = 0.0891

There was no significant difference in the way that the two groups marked this question. Both groups disagreed with the view that beta is the single most important measure of a security's risk. Sixty-eight per cent of the NIRI members marked Cell 1 or 2 (Strongly Disagree or Moderately Disagree), and 70 per cent of the CFAs marked the same way. This is a direct denial by practitioners of the CAPM (capital asset pricing model). Only 1 NIRI member (.5 per cent) marked Cell 5 (Strongly Agree) and 4 CFAs (3 per cent) marked Cell 5, or that they believe Sharpe's theory that beta is the most important risk measure.

IR/CFA IV-10:   Do you agree or disagree with the academic view that the use of index funds is the prudent way for large institutional investors to invest their funds in common stocks?

		1 Strongly Disagree	2 Moder. Disagree	3 Neutral	4 Moder. Agree	5 Strongly Agree	Totals
NIRI	Frequency	82	51	35	15	1	184
	Per Cent	44.57	27.72	19.02	8.15	0.54	
CFA	Frequency	79	46	14	7	1	147
	Per Cent	53.74	31.29	9.52	4.76	0.68	
TOTALS	Frequency	161	97	49	22	2	331
	Per Cent	48.64	29.31	14.80	6.65	0.60	

Chi-Square = 8.189   DF = 4   Prob. = 0.0849

This question showed no significant difference in the way that the two groups marked the cells. Neither group agreed with this statement. Seventy-two per cent of the NIRIs and 85 per cent of the CFAs marked either Cell 1 or 2 (Strongly Disagree or Moderately Disagree). This is not a surprising result, since both groups had rejected the CAPM (Question 9). Also, both groups' jobs depend upon the need to reject this theoretical postulate. This also lends credence to the idea that analysts believe they can spot undervalued situations, and that they believe they can always outperform the stock market averages. Only one person in each group marked Cell 5 (Strongly Agree), which says they accept indexing as the prudent way for large institutional investors to participate in common stocks.

IR/CFA IV-11:   Have you had exposure to these academic ideas, either by reading or
by experience?

		1 *Not at* *All*	*2* *Some*	*3* *A Lot*	*Totals*
NIRI	Frequency	6	91	89	186
	Per Cent	3.23	48.92	47.85	
CFA	Frequency	1	45	100	146
	Per Cent	0.68	30.82	68.49	
TOTALS	Frequency	7	136	189	332
	Per Cent	2.11	40.96	56.93	

Chi-Square = 15.171   DF = 2   Prob. = 0.0005

There is a significant difference in the way that the two groups marked
this question. The chi-square is significant at the 0.0005 level. The main difference is that the NIRIs are split approximately 50-50 between having had
"Some" exposure and "A Lot" of exposure, while the CFAs are split 1/3 to
2/3. The CFAs, through training and exams, have had more exposure to these
ideas. Interestingly, only 6 (3 per cent) of the NIRI members have had no exposure to these ideas, and only 1 CFA (0.7 per cent) had no exposure.

IR/CFA IV-12:   In the past few years, have statements such as those above affected the
way you perform your professional duties?

		1 Not at All	2 Some	3 A Lot	Totals
NIRI	Frequency	86	90	9	185
	Per Cent	46.49	48.65	4.86	
CFA	Frequency	67	65	16	148
	Per Cent	45.27	43.92	10.81	
TOTALS	Frequency	153	155	25	333
	Per Cent	45.95	46.55	7.51	

Chi-Square = 4.294   DF = 2   Prob. = 0.1169

There is no significant difference in the way that the two groups marked this question. The important point of this question, however, is that 46 per cent of the NIRIs and 45 per cent of the CFAs say that their jobs have not been affected by modern investment theory. Only 9 NIRI members said that the ideas had affected their jobs "A Lot" and only 16 CFAs responded similarly.

This response indicates that modern investment theory is still relatively new, but perhaps, as time passes, the impact on duties of these two groups will become greater. The current generation of finance students is exposed to these theoretical ideas, which should begin to show up as the students move into the financial community. However, at the present time, it appears that modern investment theory is generally rejected by practitioners.

IR IV-12 (Continued):   If your job has been affected by academic ideas, please give examples.

		No.
1.	More contact with analysts	5
2.	Approach to analysts colored by efficient markets hypothesis	4
3.	Effective communication—good and bad news	3
4.	Be aware of what information analysts desire	3
5.	Must understand latest developments to converse with analysts	3
6.	More work required	3
7.	Educate financial community to market "realities"	2
8.	Market less effective in representing intrinsic value	2
9.	Must "train" new analysts following company	1
10.	Hard to explain changes in company's stock value	1
11.	Attempt to divorce ourselves from market	1
12.	Continued efforts to raise visibility	1
13.	Hard to generate enthusiasm among analysts	1
14.	Take shifting "styles" into account in selling effort	1
15.	Encourage analysts to cover company	1
16.	Respond intelligently to market forces	1
17.	Provide statistical data to analysts	1
18.	Keep track of technical analyses	1
19.	Comment on use of "unsound" principles by analysts	1
20.	Because of rise in "indexing," sought inclusion in S&P's 500	1
21.	The need for management to maintain investor relations program	1
		38

CFA IV-12 (Continued):   If your job has been affected by academic ideas,
please give examples.

		No.
1.	Seek out "inefficient" stocks	9
2.	Too much attention paid to efficient markets hypothesis	4
3.	Changed policies to take advantage of these "new theories"	3
4.	Faddishness (fact that it is wrong) if academic views allow contrary ideas to profit	3
5.	Increased measure of risk and reward	2
6.	Performance compared to indexes	2
7.	Give clients what they want	2
8.	Avoid institutionalized securities	2
9.	Concentrated analysis on small, underanalyzed companies	2
10.	Too little attention paid to valuation	1
11.	More beta analysis	1
12.	None	1
13.	Reduced emphasis on recommendations	1
14.	"Seat of pants" valuation passe	1
15.	Only real bargains recommended	1
16.	Take advantage of others' myopia	1
17.	Less in-depth work, include broader horizon	1
18.	Harder, more competitive work	1
19.	Disclosure requirements made companies more reluctant to be open	1
20.	Individual have opportunity to capitalize on institutional "madness"	1
21.	Indexing does not require analysis of individual securities	1
22.	Consideration of technical analysis and beta	1
23.	Technical analysis useless	1
24.	Modern capital theory useless	1
25.	Easier to make money for clients who listen, harder to get institutions to listen	1
26.	Professional analysis and experience better than "fads"	1
27.	Must answer questions regarding theories	1
28.	More emphasis on accurate projections derived from computer-based data	1
29.	More quantitative work	1
30.	Broader perspective in making security evaluation	1

50

IR/CFA IV: Grouped Questions (Multi-way contingency tables).

The NIRI members and CFAs were compared on issues of broader scope than those reflected by single items within Section IV, agreement or disagreement with current academic views. The multi-way contingency table was the statistical tool used to determine whether the questionnaire provided the proper vehicle to elicit statistical differences between the sample groups.

The first two questions embody the application of the random walk theory. As previously indicated, the NIRIs and CFAs did not accept the random walk as a viable hypothesis. However, the CFAs were significantly more opposed to the theory than the NIRIs.

The second block of questions (Quesions 3, 4, 5, and 6) dealt with the semi-strong test. This area showed more favorable support from both groups. Although no significant difference was discernible between the groups (NIRI-CFA) for single items, the overall test statistic indicated a significant difference between the groups' responses. The means indicate that the CFAs evidenced stronger support for two out of the three academic views presented, and gave higher ratings overall.

Questions 7 and 8 dealt with the efficient markets hypothesis. Again, the test statistic (multi-way contingency table) indicated a difference between the two groups that was large enough to accept as not occurring by chance alone. The direction of the difference was determined again by a review of the mens. The NIRIs were more opposed to this theory, although neither group agreed with it.

In the final block of questions (Questions 9 and 10), the capital asset pricing model (CAPM) was reviewed. The analysis determined the existence of the significantly large difference between the NIRI specialists and analysts. This theory was not particularly agreeable to either group, but the CFAs expressed more opposition.

6

Summary, Conclusions, and Implications

SUMMARY OF CAPITAL MARKET ISSUES AND METHODOLOGY

The securities of public corporations are evaluated continuously by investors in the capital market. In order to ensure the efficiency of the capital market in its pricing and allocation functions, a continuing flow of useful and reliable information must reach investors in a timely fashion. At the center of this information process are the corporate investor relations specialists, who quickly disseminate useful information as it unfolds, and the security analysts, who receive and evaluate this information in terms of its effects on investment values and risks. The SEC plays a central role in determination of the content and quality of this information for the purpose of facilitating the efficiency of the capital market.

During the past 15 years, finance academicians have made the efficiency of the capital market their primary focus of study and research. This has revolutionized the field of finance theory. The emergent discipline is called "modern investment theory." It is founded on two theoretical developments: (1) the efficient markets hypothesis, which states that stock price changes follow a random walk, and thus are unpredictable; and (2) efficient portfolio diversification, which has the property of eliminating all company-specific risks, and thus leaves only market risk that cannot be diversified away. The principal implication of modern investment theory is that, by whatever device one employs, above-average returns cannot be earned consistently in the stock market—not if one uses a naive buy-hold strategy as a benchmark for his judging above-average performance. This is, of course, a direct and fundamental challenge to both market technicians and security analysts, who apparently believe they can systematically "beat the market."

The purpose of this research project was to examine the attitudes of investor relations specialists and security analysts regarding some of the issues raised by academicians in the theoretical literature about the capital market. In respect to these two groups, this research centered on: (1) the effectiveness of investor relations programs; (2) how each perceives the other in terms of job performance; (3) "hard" and "soft" information disclosures, and its significance to investment decision-making; and (4) modern investment theory as it currently is being taught in graduate business schools. These four points cover the areas of inquiry in this study, which reports the levels and differences of beliefs held by investor relations specialists and security analysts on these important capital market issues that are raised by academicians.

Rather than statistically testing a finance model, as is the usual research procedure employed in finance studies, this research effort used the survey technique, more common to marketing research, in order to discover the range of attitudes of the investor relations specialists and security analysts in the performance of their duties. Two specially designed and pre-tested questionnaires were sent to the two groups that interface each other in the capital market. The names were selected from their respective professional organizations: (1) the "in-house" investor relations specialists from the NIRI, and (2) the sell-side security analysts who hold the CFA designation from the ICFA. Data were collected by mailed questionnaire during the period June 26-July 28, 1978. The response rate was considered satisfactory from both groups: 187 replies to a mailing of 625 to the NIRI membership, for a response rate of 30 per cent, while 150 replied to a mailing of 560 of the CFAs, for a response rate of 27 per cent. No follow-up mailing of questionnaires was considered necessary.

The questionnaires primarily used a five-point scale to discern the distribution of attitudes of the respondents, ranging from "very poorly" to "very well" in response to some questions, or "strongly disagree" to "strongly agree" to others. The compiled results of the two questionnaires then were examined for the response level with respect to individual cells, or combination of cells, on the five-point scale, so that the two groups could be directly compared (in most cases) regarding their beliefs and attitudes. Further, the nonparametric chi-square (X^2) test statistic was calculated for paired responses from the compiled results, and inferences thereby drawn about the hypothesis being tested that that there was, or was not, a significant difference in the attitudes for each group relative to each specific question on the questionnaire.

It should be noted that Parts I and II of the respective questionnaires relate to how each group perceives the other in terms of job performance, and the questions asked are stated in approximately the same language for both groups. Accordingly, inferences drawn from the nonparametric tests are highly limited in applicability in these parts of the questionnaire. However, Parts III and IV of the questionnaire are identical in all respects, and are designed to elicit levels and comparative attitudes on subjects of common interest to both groups: namely, corporate-supplied information and modern investment theory. The nonparametric tests are highly significant in their application to these parts of the questionnaires.

The major conclusions drawn from the questionnaire survey are summarized below around the four major parts of the questionnaires. Although somewhat lengthy, this summary of specific conclusions that follows is justified because of the considerable amount of requested information that has not been otherwise researched in the finance literature about the two groups.

QUESTIONNAIRE CONCLUSIONS, PART I

Part I of the questionnaires is not identical for the two groups but is similar for most questions. The purpose of this set of questions is to determine the investor relations goals, the extent of their perceived achievement, and the impact of the investor relations programs on stock performance. The overall conclusion for this part of the questionnaire is that "credible communication" is the principal objective of corporate investor relations, and that companies measure up well in their accomplishing this objective. Further, stock price performance should be an important corporate objective, although it is not mentioned prominently in the statement of goals by investor relations specialists or CFAs.

More specifically, the responses to questions that match up in Part I are summarized below, with investor relations specialist perceptions discussed first, then the CFAs' perceptions.

CFA Profile

1, 2, 3. CFA. A statistical profile of the CFAs showed that about half have operating responsibility to analyze and make recommendations on the companies and industries they follow, while the remaining half hold executive positions in their sell-side investment banking and brokerage firms, in addition to their analyst responsibilities. An ever-growing group had completed the CFA exams as compared to those who completed the exams soon after 1963. Further, the CFA group surveyed are college educated, with 70 per cent holding a master's degree of some type. In short, the CFAs constitute an educated, skilled, and professional certified group.

Goals

2. IR. In terms of goals of investor relations programs, the investor relations specialists listed an understanding of the company first (57 of 249 responses). Other goals relate to increased investment interest (31 responses), keeping the investment community informed (29 responses), and a broader shareholder base (26 responses).

4. CFA. In terms of what the goals should be, CFAs favored "timely" and "reliable" information (81 or 182 responses), make the business understandable (26 responses), provide both positive and negative information (18 responses), and provide insights into management philosophies (14 responses). They showed only a slight interest in "high stock prices" (5 responses) compared with the investor relations specialists. It is important to note that the two sets of goals are by no means identical.

Goal Accomplishment

2. *IR/5. CFA.* In terms of their accomplishing the postulated goals during the past few years, both groups rated the achievement at high levels. The NIRI members rated their achievement at 74 per cent, only slightly higher than the CFAs (68 per cent). In this context, the corporations surveyed apparently feel they have done a good job ("fairly well" and "very well") in setting and accomplishing their goals, and the analysts generally confirm this attitude with respect to their information needs.

Program Activity

3. *IR/6. CFA.* In terms of activity of the investor relations programs, the CFAs and investor relations specialists rated the programs almost equally active (76 per cent), and most of this was characterized as "moderately active." The NIRI respondents saw their programs as "highly active" only by 21 per cent compared with only 15 per cent by the CFAs. Thus, there is broad agreement and moderately high ratings in these two sets of results, even though the two samples of corporations are different.

4. *IR/7. CFA.* In cultivating security analyists, the NIRI group is active at 82 percent (50 per cent consider themselves "moderately active" and 32 per cent consider themselves "highly active"), compared with CFAs, who rate the programs at 77 per cent (63 per cent "moderately active" and 14 per cent "highly active"). Again, there is broad agreement and moderately high ratings in these two sets of results.

5. *IR.* In giving examples of more aggressive investor relations efforts, the NIRIs placed primary emphasis on group analyst/brokerage meetings (67 of 208 responses), one-on-one calls on analysts and brokers (39), preparations and mailing of financial reports and "fact books" (33).

Stock Price Performance

6. *IR/8. CFA.* Regarding the importance of stock price performance as a corporate objective, the NIRI group rate it at 99 per cent (53 per cent at "average importance" and 46 per cent at "great importance") compared with 82 per cent for CFAs (56 per cent at "average importance"). However, in the statement of investor relations goals, price performance is not rated as important by CFAs, nor does it appear to be rated as highly by investor relations specialists as indicated here.

of companies on a *regular* basis to approximately 30 companies or fewer (94 per cent of respondents), with 78 of these (52 per cent) having a median of 15 companies. Only 9 analysts (6 per cent) surveyed follow over 30 companies on a regular basis. On an *irregular* basis, only 122 analysts follow 30 or fewer companies (86 per cent), and 61 of these (43 per cent) follow 10 or fewer companies. Twenty analysts (14 per cent) follow more than 30 companies on an irregular basis.

2. *CFA.* On a *combined* basis, the concentration is 30 companies or fewer (90 per cent), and the median is 15 companies (40 per cent). Thus, whether following companies on a regular or irregular basis, analysts tend to specialize in a relatively small population of companies.

Quality of Corporate Information Supplied

3a. *NIRI/2a CFA.* In another question, the analysts and investor relations specialists assesses each other on the issue of corporate information supplied that allows an understanding of the nature of the corporation's business. Each group gives the other relatively high ratings: NIRI, by 79 per cent, says analysts do a good job of understanding the nature of their business; and CFAs, by 75 per cent, say corporate investor relations specialists do a good job in supplying the information on the nature of the business.

3b. *NIRI/2b. CFA.* In providing information on operating and financial risks, each gives the other somewhat lesser marks than earned above: NIRI (71 per cent), and CFAs (58 per cent). Further, few negative marks were given by either group: NIRI (95 per cent) and CFAs (11 per cent).

3c. *NIRI/2c. CFA.* While 51 per cent of the investor relations specialists believe analysts do a good job in estimating the earnings of their client corporations, only 33 per cent of the CFAs find corporations doing a good job in supplying information for earnings estimates. The negative marks rise for both groups: NIRI (9 per cent) and CFAs (16 per cent).

3d. *NIRI/2d. CFA.* On the issue of stock valuation, the results deteriorate further. Only 37 per cent of the investor relations specialists feel analysts do a good job in estimating the value of their corporate stocks; an 53 per cent feel analysts do only an "average" job in stock valuation. On the other hand, only 20 per cent of the analysts think corporations do a good job in supplying information that assists them in the valuation process; 48 per cent see an "average" job, and 31 per cent give corporations negative marks. However, it is noteworthy that information derived from sources outside the corporation is also useful to analysts for stock valuation, and it has been estimated in the finance literature that stocks respond as much as 50 per cent to macrofactors (systematic risk) that are outside the control of corporations per se (unsystematic risk).

2e. *CFA.* An alleged common complaint by analysts is that corporations often lack candor by their failure or resistance to communicate negative developments. The questionnaire results clearly do not confirm this "complaint": only 20 per cent of the CFAs find corporations lacking in candor about negative developments; 46 per cent give favorable marks as to corporate full disclosure.

Performance Evaluation

4/5. IR. One hundred thirty-one investor relations specialists (70 per cent) found that in the category of 1-10 analysts following their companies on a regular basis, these analysts do an "excellent" overall job of evaluating their companies; and only one company marked the zero category, indicating that the NIRI specialist felt there are no analysts who do an excellent job of analyzing his company.

On the other hand, 83 investors relations specialists (50 per cent) marked the category of 1-10 analysts doing a poor overall job of evaluating their companies. Sixty-four NIRI specialists (38 per cent) marked the zero category, meaning that no analysts did a poor job. On balance, the NIRI members believe that many more analysts do an "excellent" job than those who do a "poor" job.

3/4. CFA. One hundred twenty-seven analysts (87 per cent) marked the 1-10 category (ten or fewer companies), or a median of five companies, that demonstrated excellent investor relations programs. Five analysts (3.5 per cent) felt that none of the companies they follow on a regular basis have excellent programs.

Regarding poor investor relations programs, the CFAs again marked the 1-10 category most frequently, 109, or 77 per cent, marked the zero category, suggesting that they follow no companies that have poor investor relations programs.

Many analysts commented on the questionnaire that they would not follow companies on a regular basis unless they already have good investor relations programs. Since 94 per cent of the analysts follow 30 or fewer companies on a regular basis (see Question 1, CFA), it is clear that they follow a few companies (median of five) that have poor investor relations programs, and thus, the responses do not confirm the view (noted in the comment above) that good investor relations programs must exist prior to, or as a condition of, the analyst following.

QUESTIONNAIRE CONCLUSIONS, PART III

Part III of the questionnaire surveys opinions regarding investment decision-making, of selected aspects of "hard" and "soft" information, and on the issue of information "overload." As expected, the CFAs prefer receiving more information than corporations (i.e., investor relations specialists) wish to give. The apparent reason is that security analysts constitute an "information processing industry" and do not pay for this information. Rather, corporations, who bear the costs of supplying this information, resist the trend toward additional disclosure on grounds of cost, competitive secrecy, and potential litigation. Despite this, investor relations specialists agree to the investment usefulness of selected "hard" information, while generally opposing selected "soft" information such as corporate sales and earnings forcasts.

A summary of attitudes by the two groups surveyed is as follows:

Line-of-Business

1. CFAs, by almost 97 per cent, prefer line-of-business information; and 86 per cent of the investor relations specialists agree to its importance in investment decision-making. In fact, CFAs "strongly agree" at a frequency of 86 per cent, compared with 45 per cent of NIRI membership.

Lease Capitalization

2. Lease capitalization is not as strongly felt by either group. CFAs prefer it by 57 per cent to investor relations specialists of 42 per cent. Its disutility was relatively small in both groups: 10 per cent by CFAs and 17 per cent by NIRI. Lease capitalization and line-of-business reporting are among the latest of potentially controversial issues regarding "hard" information disclosure.

Understandable Footnotes

3. Both groups, by similar response levels, agree that financial footnotes should be written in "plain English": CFAs by 71 per cent and NIRIs by 74 per cent. Despite their influence in financial reporting, certainly it is interesting that neither group is currently getting its way.

Auditor Involvement

4. Auditor involvement in quarterly reports is not particularly significant to either group; the CFAs prefer it by 40 per cent and investor relations specialists by only 26 per cent.

Auditor and Investor Relations Costs

5. Neither the CFAs nor the NIRIs find disclosure of auditors' fees important to investment decision-making.

6. Similarly, neither group finds disclosures of investor relations costs as

germane. Only about 15 per cent of the CFAs would like to see this disclosed. Investor relations costs, as well as auditors' fees, would fall under the rubric of "hard" information.

Replacement Cost Information

7. Replacement cost information, a form of "soft" information, has been a most controversial subject with corporations. Forty-six per cent of the investor relations specialists believe it is not helpful to investment decision-making, whereas 44 per cent of the CFAs believe it is. The two groups quite obviously part company on this issue.

Dividend Policy

8. Dividend policy, stated as a payout ratio, is important in investment decision-making by 77 per cent of CFAs and 56 per cent of investor relations specialists. Thus, while apparently important, it is also clear that 56 per cent of the public corporations represented in this survey do not choose to reveal this type of explicit information.

Planned Capital Expenditures

9. Both groups agree, with CFAs agreeing strongly (66 per cent), that capital expenditures planned for the next 12 months is useful information for investment decision-making: i.e., 96 per cent of the CFAs and 81 per cent of NIRIs agree to its importance.

Target Debt-Equity Ratios

10. Similarly, disclosure of target debt-equity ratios for future years also is important in decision-making. Eighty-five per cent of the CFAs and 64 per cent of the NIRI members agree. Despite its desirability, the 64 per cent of the NIRI-related corporations surveyed do not choose to disclose this information.

Management Forecasts

11. Sales forcasts, earnings, and earnings per share forecasts are the most controversial subjects of recent interest relating to "soft" information. CFAs prefer sales forecasts by 66 per cent, and 29 per cent "strongly" favor them; whereas, 38 per cent of the NIRIs favor them, while 40 per cent disagree with their importance in investment decision-making. In point of fact, very few corporations disclose their sales forecasts.

12. Management's forecast of earnings is favored 58 per cent by CFAs, 39 per cent by the NIRI members. Indeed, the NIRI group is unfavorable to earnings forecast use by approximately 50 per cent. Clearly this is an issue that divides the two groups.

13. Similarly, on earnings per share forecasts, CFAs favor by 56 per cent, and the NIRI by 37 per cent. However, the NIRIs disapprove of this suggestion by 51 per cent. The foregoing items 7-13 (Part III) are at the heart of the current controversy centering on "soft" information disclosure.

Information Overkill

14. Regarding information "overkill," investor relations specialists, by 61 per cent, feel that more information is being required of corporations by the SEC than is necessary to ensure efficient markets. Only 33 per cent of the CFAs agree with this assessment, whereas 42 per cent actually disagree with it. Again, the two groups clearly part company on this issue.

Additional Information Desired

15. When asked what further information the two groups feel would be helpful in investment decision making, the top 10 responses from each group are summarized on page 154.

QUESTIONNAIRE CONCLUSIONS, PART IV

Basic propositions and implications of modern investment theory, taught in graduate business schools for the past decade of so, were presented to CFAs and members of the NIRI for their affirmation or rejection. Overall, the two groups rejected modern investment theory, both in terms of theoretical propositions and implications for the practice of investments. However, the two groups differed on specific questionnaire results in the intensity with which they rejected the theory. Here is a summary of the specific results (the numbers match question numbers, but are used here for cross-referencing):

Random Walks

1. The idea that security price changes form a "random walk" is a central conclusion of the weak-form tests of the efficient markets hypothesis held by academicians. CFAs rejected this idea by 70 per cent, while investor relations specialists rejected it by 60 per cent.

2. The random walk hypothesis further states that the work of "technicians" (knowledge of historical patterns of stock prices) does not aid investors in

	NIRI			CFA	
1.	Segment reporting	(5)	1.	Segment reporting	(17)
2.	Information of strategy, goals and objectives	(5)	2.	Industry trends	(6)
3.	Nothing more needed	(5)	3.	Market share data	(4)
4.	Forecasts	(4)	4.	Evaluation of competitive position	(4)
5.	Cost of, effect of, government compliance	(3)	5.	Competitive impact of major developments	(4)
6.	Market share data	(3)	6.	All currency effects	(3)
7.	ROE and ROI goals	(3)	7.	Better information on problem areas	(3)
8.	Management succession and development	(2)	8.	Long-term corporate goals	(3)
9.	Management experience and background	(2)	9.	Pricing policy	(3)
10.	Capital expenditure allocations	(2)	10.	Pension costs	(2)

the attainment of improved investor performance (i.e., in making above-normal returns vis-a-vis a naive buy-hold strategy). Both groups reject this: 55 per cent by CFAs, and 45 per cent by investor relations specialists. However, their intensity of rejection is not as strong as that of the "random walk" proposition (Part IV-Question1). In fact, it is interesting that 36 per cent of the investor relations specialists and 26 per cent of the CFAs actually agree with the conclusion that "charting" is apparently useless.

Efficient Markets Hypothesis

3. The semi-strong form tests of the efficient markets hypothesis focuses on the rapidity with which subsets of information are discounted by the market, and concludes, in principle, that such information is discounted very rapidly. In this sense of an efficient market, both groups agree: 70 per cent (NIRI) and 64 per cent (CFA). However, this response is in conflict with those of Questions 1 and 2: if the market discounts information quickly, finance theory holds there

are not sufficient time-lags or dependency effects (serial correlation in the numbers) for technicians to produce above-average investment returns.

4. An even stronger statement made by the efficient markets hypothesis is that the market, in discounting information, does so correctly (i.e., stock prices at any given time are good estimates of fundamental values). Both groups of respondents to the questionnaire reject this statement: 60 per cent by the CFAs and 67 per cent by the NIRIs. By implication, both groups agree that stocks often depart from "equilibrium values" (are undervalued or overvalued). If the statement from finance theory is true, and both groups agreed with it, there would be serious questions about the utility of fundamental analysis as practiced by security analysts.

Stock Splits

While 52 per cent of the investor relations specialists moderately agree that stock splits raise the value of corporate shares, only 39 per cent of CFAs reveal the same conclusion. Modern investment theory holds that stock splits are fully discounted by the declaration date, and thus, no favorable price action is likely after that point.

News Dissemination

6. Both groups appear to believe that "good news" is disseminated more promptly than "bad news" by corporations. CFAs are somewhat more intense in this view (66 per cent) than investor relations specialists (59 per cent). However, this disparity in news dissemination (between "good" and "bad" news) raises some questions about the efficiency of the market.

Value of Security Analysis

7. That security analysis is "logically incomplete and valueless" is an implication of modern investment theory and a direct challenge to security analysts. However, this view is rejected by both groups: 68 per cent by CFAs, and 76 per cent by investor relations specialists. To some extent, the NIRIs see security analysis as more important or valuable than do CFAs.

Analyst Population

8. Also, both groups reject the idea that there are more security analysts than are needed to keep the stock market efficient: 62 per cent rejection by NIRIs and 44 per cent by CFAs. However, one is surprised by the lack of strong affirmation of CFAs of their own profession.

Beta and Indexing

9. Beta, or systematic risk, goes to the heart of portfolio theory and the capital asset pricing model. Modern investment theory states that, through efficient diversification, only systematic risk remains to be compensated for. Both groups deny this article of academic faith: 68 per cent rejection by the NIRI members and 70 per cent by CFAs.

10. If beta analysis captured the risks inherent in equity investment, then indexing (using "index" funds) would be the appropriate method of investment for large institutional investors. However, this academic view is decisively rejected: 72 per cent by the NIRI and 85 per cent by CFAs—a logical response since the livelihood of both groups would be brought into questions.

Exposure and Effects of Modern Investment Theory

11. The ideas of modern investment theory, as expressed in statements 1 through 10 in Part IV, are known to both groups: 99 per cent to CFAs, and 97 per cent to the members of the NIRI. However, CFAs have ("a lot") more exposure (68.5 per cent) than the case of the NIRI members (48 per cent). This is not surprising, since CFAs must be quite familiar with these ideas in order to pass their examinations for the CFA designation.

12. Both groups have felt "some" impact of these ideas (49 per cent for NIRI; 44 per cent for CFAs), whereas about an equal distribution have felt no impact at all on their professional duties (46.5 per cent for NIRI; 45 per cent for CFAs). However, the responses to how these ideas have impacted their professional duties are not particularly edifying.

IMPLICATIONS OF RESEARCH FINDINGS

In Part I of the questionnaire, the investor relations goals and extent of their achievement are broadly supported by both groups. Therefore, no major indictment or alteration of investor relations programs seems in order. However, the issue of stock price performance is ambiguously perceived by both groups in the questionnaire results. This raises the central question of what should be the role of stock price performance as a corporate investor relations objective. Modern investment theory would conclude that, since the capital market is efficient in the assessment of corporate values, it would be a redundant and expensive exercise for corporations to attempt to influence stock prices through their investor relations programs. If this view ultimately should prevail, then investor relations programs would need to be altered so they merely supply timely information through various communications media, and those programs whose purpose is to influence stock prices (such as aggressive and expensive contacts with various analyst and stockbroker groups) should be eliminated. However, while not affecting stock prices, this would be difficult for corporations to do, since analysts seem to favor this kind of an investor relations approach.

One other point is worth noting. Most investor relations specialists believe that their companies' stocks are undervalued. This belief is in direct opposition to the view held by financial academicians—a widely held but not universal view—that stock prices at any given time are in equilibrium (that is, correctly or "fully" priced). Any aggressive effort by investor relations programs to influence stock prices would shift prices away from their equilibrium values, and this would have the effect of producing inefficiencies in the capital market, a situation not welcomed by the SEC.

Responses to Part II of the questionnaire show clearly that the two groups differ substantially on the quality of corporate disclosure that enables security analysts to estimate future corporate earnings and investment values. In fact, it is ironic that most investor relations specialists believe analysts do a good job in projecting earnings, while analysts, in turn, do not feel that corporations have supplied them with sufficient information to make this estimate accurately. Clearly analysts perceived a deficiency in investor relations programs that hampers the analysts' bottom-line performance: namely, in estimating earnings and investment values.

This apparent conflict is further amplified in Part III of the questionnaire. Analysts perceive a need for more corporate information than corporations wish to reveal, and particularly in the area of "soft" information. Almost certainly, pressures will build that eventually will force corporations to provide the desired information, since in fact, analysts and the SEC see eye-to-eye on the particular issue. However, there is agreement among some finance academicians (cited in Chapter 3) and investor relations specialists that more corporate information is now being supplied than is necessary to ensure efficient markets. Further research into this important and interesting area is warranted. Beaver (see Chapter 3) believes it would be beneficial, for SEC policy-making, if researchers assessed specific information disclosures (e.g., specific FASBs) on the basis of a cost-benefit analysis. Nothing of this sort has been done in the financial research literature. Yet it would illuminate an important economic issue—that information, like any other product or service, is amenable to economic analysis, and that, to be economically viable, its benefits should exceed its costs.

Finally, the questions raised in Part IV of the questionnaire are extremely controversial. Modern investment theory, as one can see, is soundly rejected, while both groups also indicated general familiarity with its content and implications. While the specific propositions and implications of modern investment theory will not be detailed here again (see Chapter 4), if this view should be generally accepted, it would have profound and far-reaching effects on the institutional characteristics of investment practices. Institutionally, it would imply the following: (1) fewer technicians—perhaps none at all; (2) fewer security analysts; (3) a scaling down of investor relations programs; (4) relaxation of disclosure requirements; (5) investments viewed in a portfolio context, and not in terms of individual stock analysis; (6) funds more passively invested—such as in "index" funds"; and (7) a general re-orientation of the investment world away from the view that investors can beat the market. If this view should prevail, Wall Street will never be the same!

Notes

Chapter 2

1. Kennedy, Robert E., Speech to Baldor Electric Company District Managers, Fort Smith, Arkansas, October 1977.

2. Laporte, Lowell. *Investor Relations,* Studies in Business Policy, No. 124. New York: National Industrial Conference Board, 1967, p. 49.

3. Ibid., p. 49.

4. Weston, J. Fred. *The Scope and Methodology of Finance,* Foundations of Finance Series. Englewood Cliffs, N.J.: Prentice-Hall, Inc., 1966, p. 88.

5. Report of the Advisory Committee on Corporate Disclosure to the SEC. Washington, D.C.: Government Printing Office, 1976, quoted in: William H. Beaver, "Current Trends in Corporate Disclosure," *Journal of Accountancy,* Vol. 145, No. 1 (January 1978), 45.

6. Ibid.

7. New York Stock Exchange, *Expanded Policy on Timely Disclosure,* reprinted from New York Stock Exchange Manual (October 1969), A-18.

8. Ibid., A-28.

9. Ibid.

10. Garrett, Ray, Jr., "The Role of Financial Public Relations," Address presented to the Publicity Club of Chicago, March 13, 1974, Chicago, Illinois, p. 3.

11. Fisher, Irving, Kemmerer, Edwin Walter, Brown, Harry G., and others, *How to Invest When Prices Are Rising.* Scranton, Pa.: G. L. Sumner and Co., 1912.

12. Smith, E. L., *Common Stocks as Long-Run Investments.* New York: The Macmillan Company, 1924.

13. Graham, Benjamin and Dodd, David L., *Security Analysis.* New York:McGraw-Hill Book Company, Inc., 1934.

14. Ibid.

15. Ibid., p. 1.

16. Ibid., p. 13.

17. Ibid., p. 14.

18. Ibid., p. 14.

19. Ibid., p. 21.

20. Ibid., pp. 21-22.

21. Norby, William C., "Overview of Financial Analysis," in *Financial Analysts Handbook*. Homewood, Ill.: Dow Jones-Irwin, 1975, p. 4.

22. Ibid., p. 5.

23. Brodrick, Richard M., "Introduction-Appendix," *Investor Relations Handbook*. AMA-COM, 1974, 182.

24. Chatlos, William, "What is Investor Relations," *Investor Relations Handbook*. AMA-COM, 1974, 4.

25. Beaver, William H., "Current Trends in Corporate Disclosure," The Journal of Accountancy, Vol. 145, No. 1 (January, 1978), 45.

26. NIRI, A Perspective on Investor Relations, July 1979, p. 4-9.

27. Ibid., p. 4.

28. NIRI, A Broad-Based Study of the Investor Relations Profession, March, 1974, p. 47.

29. Ibid., pp. 51, 55.

30. NIRI, 1978 Membership Directory, inside front cover.

31. Ibid., p. 93.

32. Ibid., inside back cover.

33. ICFA, 1977-1978 Directory of Members, p. 5.

34. Ibid., p. 24.

35. Norby, p. 22.

36. Williams, William D., "FAF Corporate Information Committee Awards for Excellence in Corporate Reporting for 1976," *Financial Analysts Federation, Vol. 34, No. 1 (Jan.-Feb., 1978), p. 42.*

Chapter 3

1. Beaver, William H. "Current Trends in Corporate Disclosure," *The Journal of Accountancy,* Vol. 145, No. 1 (January 1978), 45.

2. Robbins, H. Zane. "Your New Quarterly Report," *Public Relations Journal,* Vol. 32, No. 4 (April 1976), 24.

3. Beaver, p. 48.

4. Ibid., p. 46.

5. Gray, William S., III. "Proposal for Systematic Disclosure of Corporate Forecasts," *Financial Analysts Journal,* Vol. 29, No. 1 (January/February 1973), 67-68.

6. Bissell, George S. "A Professional Investor Looks at Earnings Forecasts," *Financial Analysts Journal,* Vol. 28, No. 3 (May/June 1972), 73.

7. Barnea, Amir, Sadan, Simcha, and Schiff, Michael. "Afraid of Publishing Forecasts?" *Financial Executive,* Vol. XLV, No. 11 (November 1977), 57.

8. Kapnick, Harvey E. "Will Financial Forecasts Really Help Investors," *Financial Executive,* Vol. XL, No. 8 (August 1972), 52.

9. Fuller, Russell J. and Metcalf, Richard W. "Management Disclosures: Analysts Prefer Facts to Management's Predictions," *Financial Analysts Journal,* Vol. 34, No. 2 (March/April 1978), 57.

10. Beaver, p. 52.

11. Laffer, Arthur B. "Do Investors Need More Information?" *The Attack on Corporate America,* M. Bruce Johnson, ed. New York: McGraw-Hill, Inc., 1978, pp. 109-110.

Chapter 4

1. Bachelier, Louis. "Theory of Speculation," in *The Random Character of Stock Market Prices.* Cambridge: MIT Press, 1964, pp. 17-78.

2. Working, Holbrook. "A Random-Difference Series for Use in the Analysis of Time Series," *Journal of the American Statistical Association* (March 1934), Vol. 29, No. 185, pp. 11-24.

3. Cowles, Alfred, and Jones, Herbert F. "Some a Posteriori Probabilities in Stock Market Action," *Econometrica* (July 1937), Vol. 5, No. 3, pp. 280-94.

4. Kendall, Maurice G. "The Analysis of Economic Time-Series—Part I: Prices," *Journal of the Royal Statistical Society* (1953), Vol. 96, Pt. I, pp. 11-25.

5. Osborne, M. F. M. "Brownian Motion in the Stock Market," *Operations Research* (March-April 1959), Vol. 7, No. 2, pp. 145-73.

6. Kendall, op. cit.

7. Osborne, op. cit.

8. Granger, Clive W. J. and Morgenstern, Oskar. "Spectral Analysis of New York Stock Market Prices," *Kyklos* (1963), Vol. 16, pp. 1-27.

9. Fama, Eugene F. "The Behavior of Stock Market Prices," *Journal of Business* (January 1965), Vol. 38, No. 1, pp. 34-105.

10. Fama, Eugene F. "Efficient Capital Markets: A Review of Theory and Empirical Work," *Journal of Finance* (May 1970), Vol. 25, No. 2, pp. 383-417.

11. Roberts, Harry V. "Stock Market Patterns and Financial Analysis: Methodological Suggestions," *Journal of Finance* (March 1959), Vol. XIV, No. 1, pp. 1-10.

12. Cheng, Pao L. and Deets, M. King. "Portfolio Returns and the Random Walk Theory," *Journal of Finance* (March 1971), Vol. 26, No. 1, pp. 11-30.

13. Shiskin, Julius. "Systematic Aspects of Stock Price Fluctuations," University of Chicago, Seminar on the Analysis of Security Prices, May 1968.

14. Alexander, Sidney S. "Price Movement in Speculative Markets: Trends or Random Walks," *Industrial Management Review* (May 1961), Vol. 2, No. 2, 7-26.

15. Cootner, Paul H. "Random Character of Stock Market Prices," *Industrial Management Review* (Spring 1962), Vol. 3, No. 2, pp. 24-45.

16. Levy, Robert A. "Random Walks: Reality or Myth," *Financial Analysts Journal* (November/December 1967), Vol. 23, No. 6, pp. 69-76.

17. Jensen, Michael C. and Bennington, George A., "Random Walks and Technical Theories: Some Additional Evidence," *Journal of Finance* (May 1970), Vol. 25, No. 2, pp. 460-82.

18. Jen, Frank C. "Discussion," *Journal of Finance* (May 1970), Vol. 25, No. 2, pp. 495-99.

19. Kruizenga, Richard J. "Profit Returns from Purchasing Puts and Calls," in Paul H. Cootner, "Random Character of Stock Market Prices."

20. Boness, A. James. "Some Evidence on the Profitability of Trading in Puts and Calls," in Paul H. Cootner, "Random Character of Stock Market Prices," pp. 475-96.

21. Levy, op. cit., pp. 69-76.

22. Fama, Eugene F. "Efficient Capital Markets," *Journal of Finance* (May 1970), Vol. 25, No. 2, pp. 383-417.

23. Fama, Eugene F. "The Behavior of Stock Market Prices," *Journal of Business* (January 1965), Vol. 38, no. 1.

24. Fama, Eugene F. "Random Walks Walks in Stock Market Prices," *Financial Analysts Journal* (September/October, 1965), Vol. 21, No. 5, pp. 55-59.

25. Graham, Benjamin, Dodd, David L., and Cottle, Sidney. *Security Analysis: Principles and Technique,* 4th edition. New York: McGraw-Hill Book Company, 1962, p. 711.

26. Lorie, James H., and Hamilton, Mary T. *The Stock-Market—Theories and Evidence* Homewood, Ill.: Richard D. Irwin, Inc., 1973), p. 81.

27. Fama, Eugene F., Fisher, Lawrence, Jensen, Michael C., and Roll, Richard. "The Adjustment of Stock Prices to New Information," *International Economic Review* (February 1969), Vol. 10, No. 1, pp. 1-21.

28. Ibid.

29. Fama, Eugene F. "Efficient Captial Markets," *Journal of Finance* (May 1970), Vol. 25, No. 2., p. 405.

30. Ibid., pp. 407-408.

31. Ball, Ray, and Brown, Philip. "An Empirical Evaluation of Accounting Income," *Journal of Accounting Research* (Autumn 1968), Vol. 6, No. 2, pp. 159-78.

32. Neiderhoffer, Victor, and Regan, Patrick J. "Earnings Changes, Analysts Forecasts and Stock Prices," *Financial Analysts Journal* (May/June 1972), Vol. 28, No. 3, pp. 69-74.

33. Lorie, James H., and Hamilton, Mary T. p.100.

34. Wallich, Henry C. "What Does the Random Walk Hypothesis Mean to Security Analysts?" *Financial Analysts Journal* (March/April 1968), Vol. 24, No. 2, pp. 159-62.

35. Diefenback, Robert E. "How Good Is Institutional Brokerage Research," *Financial Analysts Journal* (January/February 1972), Vol. 28, No. 1, pp. 55-60.

36. Friend, Irwin, Blume, Marshall, and Crockett, Jean. *Mutual Funds and Other Institutional Investors,* Twenty Century Fund Study. New York: McGraw-Hill Book Company, 1970.

37. Miller, Paul F., Jr. *Institutional Service Report—Monthly Review* Philadelphia: Drexel and Co., Inc., November 1965.

38. Wallich, Henry C. "Traditional vs. Performance Stock Valuation," *Commercial and Financial Chronicle* (February 18, 1971), pp. 1-5.

39. Kuehner, Charles D. "Efficient Markets and Random Walk," *Financial Analysts Handbook,* Vol. 1 Homewood, Ill.: Dow Jones-Irwin, 1975.

40. Markowitz, Harry. *Portfolio Selection: Efficient Diversification of Investments.* New York: John Wiley, 1959, p. 3.

41. Ibid., p. 5.

42. Sharpe, William F. *Portfolio Theory and Capital Markets.* New York:McGraw-Hill Book Company, 1970, pp. 118-22.

43. Sharpe, William F. *Investments.* Englewood Cliffs, N. J.: Prentice-Hall, Inc., 1978, p. 118.

44. Ibid., p. 119.

45. Sharpe, William F. *Portfolio Theory and Capital Markets,* p. 83.

46. Blume, Marshall E., and Friend, Irwin. "A New Look at the Capital Asset Pricing Model," *Journal of Finance* (March 1973), Vol. 28, No. 1, pp. 19-33.

47. Jensen, Michael C. "Capital Markets: Theory and Evidence," *The Bell Journal of Economics and Management Science* (Autumn 1972), Vol. 3, No. 2, pp. 167-247.

48. Jacob, Nancy. "The Measurement of Systematic Risk for Securities and Portfolios: Some Empirical Evidence," *Journal of Financial and Quantitative Analysis* (March 1971), Vol. 6, No. 2, pp. 815-34.

49. Miller, Merton H., and Scholes, Myron S. "Rates of Return in Relation to Risk: A Reexamination of Recent Findings," in *Studies in the Theory of Capital Markets,* New York: Praeger Publishers, Inc., 1972, pp. 47-48, quoted by Franco Modigliani and Gerald A. Pogue, "An Introduction to Risk and Return: Concepts and Evidence," *Financial Analysts Handbook,* Vol. 1 Homewood, Illinois: Dow Jones-Irwin, 1975, pp. 1330-31.

50. Friend, Irwin and Blume, Marshall E. "Risk and the Long Run Rate of Return on NYSE Common Stocks," quoted by Franco Modigliani and Gerald A. Pogue, "An Introduction to Risk and Return: Concepts and Evidence," *Financial Analysts Handbook,* Vol, 1 Homewood, Illinois: Dow Jones-Irwin, 1975.

51. Black, Fisher, Jensen, Michael C., and Scholes, Myron S. "The Capital Asset Pricing Model: Some Empirical Tests," in *Studies in the Theory of Capital Markets.* New York: Praeger Publishers, Inc. 1972, pp. 79-121.

52. Fama, Eugene F. and MacBeth, James D. "Risk Return and Equilibrium: Empirical Tests," *Journal of Political Economy* (May/June 1973), Vol. 81, No. 3, pp. 607-36, quoted by Franco Modigliani and Gerald A. Pogue, "An Introduction to Risk and Return: Concepts and Evidence," *Financial Analysts Handbook,* Vol. 1. Homewood, Illinois: Dow Jones-Irwin, 1975, pp. 1334-35.

53. Lintner, John. "The Valuation of Risk Assets and the Selection of Risky Investments in Stock Portfolios and Capital Budgets," *Review of Economics and Statistics* (February 1965), Vol. 47, No. 1, pp. 13-37.

54. Levy, Robert A. "On the Short Term Stationarity of Beta Coefficients," *Financial Analysts Journal* (November/December 1971), Vol. 27, No. 6, pp. 55-62.

55. Modigliani, Franco, and Pogue, Gerald R. "An Introduction to Risk and Return: Concepts and Evidence," *Financial Analysts Handbook*, Vol. 1. Homewood Illinois: Dow Jones-Irwin, 1975, pp. 1135-36.

Chapter 5

1. Barr, Anthony J., Goodnight, James H., Sall, John P., and Helwig, Jane T. *A User's Guide to SAS-76*. Raleigh, N. C.: Sparks Press, 1976.

2. Siegel, Sidney. *Non-Parametric Statistics for the Behavioral Sciences*. New York: McGraw-Hill Book Company, 1956, pp. 104-11.

3. Joselyn, Robert W. *Designing the Marketing Research Project*. Lexington, N. Y.: Petrocelli/Charter, Inc., 1977, p. 140.

4. Modigliani, Franco and Miller, Merton H. "Corporate Income Tax as the Cost of Capital: A Correction," *American Economic Review* (June 1963), Vol. 13, No. 3, pp. 433-43.

5. Fama, Eugene, Fisher, Laurence, Jensen, Michael C., and Roll, Richard. "The Adjustment of Stock Prices to New Information," *International Economic Review* (February 1969), Vol. 10, No. 1, pp. 1-21.

Bibliography

Alexander, Sidney S. "Price Movement in Speculative Markets: Trends of Random Walks," *Industrial Management Review* (May 1961), Vol. 2, No. 2, pp. 7-26.

Appleman, Mark J. "The Three Minds of the Money Manager, " *Financial Analysts Journal* (September/October 1973), Vol. 29, No. 5, pp. 49-54.

Bachelier, Louis. "Theory of Speculation," in *The Random Character of Stock Market Prices.* Cambridge: MIT Press, 1964, pp. 17-18.

Ball, Ray, and Brown, Philip. "An Empirical Evaluation of Accounting Income Numbers," *Journal of Accounting Research* (Autumn 1968), Vol. 6, No. 2, pp. 159-78.

Barnea, Amir, and Brenner, M. "World Events and Stock Market Volume," *Financial Analysts Journal* (July/August 1974), Vol. 30, No. 4, pp. 64-67.

_____., and Logue, Dennis E. "Evaluating the Forecasts of a Security Analyst," *Financial Management* (Summer 1973), Vol. 2, No. 2, pp. 38-45.

_____ . , Sadan Simcha, and Schiff, Michael. "Afraid of Publishing Forecasts?" *Financial Executive* (November 1977), Vol. XLV, No. 11, pp. 52-57.

Barr, Anthony J., Sall, John P., Goodnight, James H., and Helwig, Jane T. *A User's Guide to Sas-76.* Raleigh, N. C.: Sparks Press, 1976.

Bar-Yosef, Sasson, and Brown, Lawrence D. "A Reexamination of Stock Splits Usins Moving Betas," *Journal of Finance* (September 1977), Vol. 32, No. 4, pp. 1069-80.

Basu, S. "The Investment Performance of Common Stocks in Relation to Their Price-Earning Ratios: A Test of the Efficient Market Hypothesis," *Journal of Finance* (June 1977), Vol. 32, No. 3, pp. 663-82.

Baumol, William F. *The Stock Market and Economic Efficiency.* Bronx, New York: Fordham University Press, 1965.

Bawa, Vijay S. "A New Look at the Capital Asset Pricing Model," *Methodology in Finance—Investments.* Lexington, Mass.: Lexington Books, 1972.

Beaver, Willian H. "Current Trends in Corporate Disclosure." *Journal of Accountancy* (January, 1978), Vol. 145, No. 1, pp. 44-52.

Beja, Aveaham. "On Systematic and unsystematic components of financial Risk," *Journal of Finance* (March, 1972), Vol. 27, No. 1, pp. 37-45.

Bevis, Herman W. *Corporate Financial Reporting in a Competitive Economy.* New York: The Macmillan Company, 1965.

Bicksler, James L. "The Coming Revolution in Investment Management," *Methodology in Finance—Investments.* Lexington, Mass.: Lexington Books, 1972.

Bissell, George S. "A Professional Investor Looks at Earnings Forecasts," *Financial Analysts Journal* (May/June 1972), Vol. 28, No. 3, pp. 73-78.

Black, Fisher. "The Investment Policy Spectrum," *Financial Analysts Journal* (January-February 1976), Vol. 32, No. 1, pp. 23-31.

_____ ., Jensen, Michael C., and Scholes, Myron S. "The Capital Asset Pricing Model: Some Empirical Tests," in *Studies in the Theory of Capital Markets.* New York: Praeger Publishers, Inc., 1972, pp. 79-121.

Blume, Marshall E. "Betas and Their Regression Tendencies," *Journal of Finance* (June 1975), Vol. 30, No. 3, pp. 785-95.

_____ . "On the Assessment of Risk," *Journal of Finance* (March 1971), Vol. 26, No. 1, pp. 1-10.

────── . "Portfolio Theory: A Step Toward Its Practical Application," *Journal of Business* (April 1970), Vol. 43, No. 2, pp. 152-73.

────── ,. and Friend, Irwin. "A New Look at the Captial Asset Pricing Model," *Journal of Finance* (March, 1973), Vol. 28, No. 1, pp. 19-33.

────── ., and Husic, Frank. "Price, Beta, and Exchange Listing," *Journal of Finance* (May 1973), Vol. 28, No. 2, pp. 283-99.

Boness, A. James. "Some Evidence on the Profitability of Trading in Puts and Calls," in Paul J. Cootner, "Random Character of Stock Market Prices," *Industrial Management Review* (Spring, 1962), Vol. 3, No. 2, pp. 475-96.

Brealy, Richard A. *An Introduction to Risk and Return from Common Stocks.* Cambridge, Mass.: MIT Press, 1969.

────── . *Security Prices in a Competitive Market.* Cambridge, Mass.: MIT Press, 1971.

Brodrick, Richard M., ed. *Investor Relations Handbook.* American Management Association, 1974.

Brown, Marilyn. "Corporate Reporting in a Changing Environment," *Public Relations Journal* (April 1976), Vol. 32, No. 4, pp. 14-15.

Carlson, Robert S. "Aggregate Performance of Mutual Funds, 1948-67," *Journal of Financial and Quantitative Analysis* (March 1970), Vol. 5, No. 1, pp. 1-32.

Chamberlain, Lawrence, and Hay, William Wren. *Investment and Speculation.* New York: Henry Holt, 1931.

Chatlos, William. "What Is Investor Relations," *Investor Relations Handbook.* American Management Association, 1974.

Cheng, Pao L., and Deets, M. King. "Portfolio Returns and the Random Walk Theory," *Journal of Finance* (March 1971), Vol. 26, No. 1, pp. 11-30.

Cooley, Philip L. "A Multidimensional Analysis of Institutional Investor Perception of Risk," *Journal of Finance* (March 1977), Vol. 32, No. 1, pp. 67-68.

Cooper, Richard V. L. "Efficient Capital Markets and the Quantity Theory of Money," *Journal of Finance* (June 1974), Vol. 29, No. 3, pp. 887-908.

Cootner, Paul H. "Random Character of Stock Market Prices," *Industrial Management Review* (Spring 1962), Vol. 3, No. 2, pp. 24-45.

────── . "Stock Prices: Random Vs. Systematic Changes," *Industrial Management* (Spring 1962), Vol. 3, No. 2, pp. 24-45.

Coplin, Robert A. "Marketing Concepts Can Improve Your Investor Relations," *Financial Executive* (November 1977), Vol. 45, No. 11, pp. 32-35.

Cowles, Alfred, and Jones, Herbert F. "Some a Posteriori Probabilities in Stock Market Action," *Econometrica* (July 1937), Vol. 5, No. 3, pp. 280-94.

Cragg, John G., and Malkiel, Burton G. "The Concensus and Accuracy of Some Predictions of the Growth of Corporate Earnings," *Journal of Finance* (March 1968), Vol. 23, No. 1, pp. 67-84.

Crowell, Richard A. "Five Applications of Beta," *Financial Analysts Journal* (July/August 1973), Vol. 29, No. 4, pp. 81-87.

Dennis, Charles N. "An Investigation into the Effects of Independent Investor Relations Firms on Common Stock Prices," *Journal of Finance* (May 1973), Vol. 28, No. 3, pp. 373-80.

Diefenback, Robert E. "How Good Is Institutional Brokerage Research," *Financial Analysts Journal* (January/February 1972), Vol. 28, No. 1, pp. 55-60.

Drzycimski, Eugene F., and Yudelson, Julian E. "Problems in the Measurement of Risk," *Financial Executive* (September 1969), Vol. 37, No. 9, pp. 32-36.

Durand, David. "Growth Stocks and the Petersburg Paradox," *Journal of Finance* (September 1957), Vol. 12, No. 3, pp. 348-63.

Dyl, Edward A. "Capital Gains Taxation and Year-End Stock Market Behavior" *Journal of Finance* (March 1977), Vol. 32, No. 1, pp. 165-75.

Ellis, Charles D. "A Conversation with Benjamin Graham," *Financial Analysts Journal* (September/October 1976), Vol. 32, No. 5, pp. 20-24.

────── . *Institutional Investing.* Homewood, Ill.: Dow Jones-Irwin, 1971.

Elton, Edwin J., Gruber, Martin J., and Urich, Thomas J. "Are Betas Best," *Journal of*

Finance (December 1978), Vol. 33, No. 5, pp. 1375-84.

Emery, John T. "Efficient Capital Markets and the Information Content of Accounting Numbers," *Journal of Financial and Quantitative Analysis* (March 1974), Vol. 9, No. 2, pp. 139-50.

_____ . "The Information Content of Daily Market Indicators," *Journal of Financial and Quantitative Analysis* (March 1973), Vol. 8, No. 2, pp. 183-90.

Evans, John L. and Archer, Stephen H. "Diversification and the Reduction of Dispersion," *Journal of Finance* (December 1968), Vol. 23, No. 5, pp. 761-68.

Expanded Policy on Timely Disclosure. New York Stock Exchange, reprinted from New York Stock Exchange Manual (October 1969), p. A-18.

Fabozzi, Frank J., and Francis, Jack Clark. "Beta as a Random Coefficient," *Journal of Financial and Quantitative Analysis* (March 1978), Vol. 13, No. 1, pp. 101-16.

Fama, Eugene F. "The Adjustment of Stock Prices to New Information," *International Economic Review* (June 1968), Vol. 9, No. 2.

_____ . "The Behavior of Stock Market Prices," *Journal of Business* (January 1965), Vol. 38, No. 1, pp. 34-105.

_____ . "Efficient Capital Markets: A Review of Theory and Empirical Work," *Journal of Finance* (May 1970), Vol. 25, No. 2, pp. 383-417.

_____ . *Foundations of Finance.* New York: Basic Books, 1976.

_____ . "Mandelbrot and the Stable Paretian Hypothesis," *Journal of Business* (October 1963), Vol. 36, No. 4, pp. 420-29.

_____ . "Random Walks in Stock Market Prices," *Financial Analysts Journal* (September/October 1965), Vol. 21, No. 5, pp. 55-59.

_____ . "Risk, Return and Equilibrium," *Journal of Political Economy* (January/February 1971), Vol. 79, No. 1, pp. 30-55.

_____ ., and Blume, Marshall. "Filter Rules and Stock Market Trading Profits," *Journal of Business* (Special Supplement) (January 1966), Vol. 39, No. 1, pp. 226-41.

_____ ., Fisher, Lawrence, Jensen, Michael C., and Roll, Richard. "The Adjustment of Stock Prices to New Information," *International Economic Review* (February 1969), Vol. 10, No. 1, pp. 1-21.

_____ ., and Laffer, Arthur B. "Information and Capital Markets," *Journal of Business* (July 1971), Vol. 44, No. 3, pp. 289-98.

_____ ., and MacBeth, James D. "Risk Return and Equilibrium: Empirical Tests." *Journal of Political Economy* (May/June 1973), Vol. 81, No. 3, pp. 607-36, quoted by Franco Modigliani and Gerald A. Pogue, "An Introduction to Risk and Return: Concepts and Evidence," *Financial Analysts Handbook,* Vol. 1 (Homewood, Ill.: Dow Jones-Irwin, 1975), pp. 1334-35.

Ferguson, Robert. "Do Inventory Funds Make Sense?" *Financial Analysts Journal* (May/June 1978), Vol. 34, No. 3, pp. 38-45.

_____ . "How to Beat the Index Funds," *Financial Analysts Journal* (May/June 1975), Vol. 31, No. 3, pp. 63-72.

Fewings, David. "The Impact of Growth on the Risk of Common Stocks," *Journal of Finance* (May 1975), Vol. 30, No. 2, pp. 525-31.

Finnerty, Joseph E. "The CBOE and Market Efficiency," *Journal of Financial and Quantitative Analysis* (March 1978), Vol. 13, No. 1, pp. 29-38.

_____ . "Insider's Activity and Inside Information: A Multivariate Analysis," *Journal of Financial and Quantitative Analysis* (June 1976), Vol. 11, No. 2, pp. 205-36.

_____ . "Insiders and Market Efficiency," *Journal of Finance* (September 1976), Vol. 31, No. 4, pp. 1141-48.

Fisher, Irving. *How to Invest When Prices Are Rising.* New York: The Macmillan Company, 1912.

Fisher, Lawrence. "Analysts' Input and Portfolio Changes," *Financial Analysts Journal* (May/June 1975), Vol. 31, No. 3, pp. 73-85.

_____ . "Outcome for Random Investments in Common Stocks on the NYSE," *Journal of Business* (April 1965), Vol. 38, No. 2, pp. 149-61.

_____ ., and Lorie, James H. "Rates of Return on Investments in Common Stocks," *Journal of Business* (January 1964), Vol. 37, No. 1, pp. 1-21.

Foster, LeBaron R. "Telling the Company's Financial Story." Financial Executives Research Foundation. New York, 1964.

Francis, Jack Clark and Archer, Stephen H. *Portfolio Analysis.* Englewood Cliffs, N. J.: Prentice-Hall, Foundations of Finance Series, 2nd edition, 1979.

Frankfurter, George M. "Ex-Post Performance of the Sharpe Portfolio Selection Model," *Journal of Finance* (June 1976), Vol. 31, No. 3, pp. 949-55.

Friend, Irwin, and Blume, Marshall E. "Risk and the Long Run Rate of Return on NYSE Common Stocks," quoted by Franco Modigliani and Gerald A. Pogue, "An Introduction to Risk and Return: Concepts and Evidence," *Financial Analysts Handbook,* Vol. 1. Homewood, Ill.: Dow Jones-Irwin, 1975, pp. 1332-33.

——————., Blume, Marshall, and Crockett, Jean. *Mutual Funds and Other Institutional Investors,* a Twenty Century Fund Study. New York: McGraw-Hill, 1970.

——————., Westerfield, Randolph, and Granito, Michael. "New Evidence on the CAPM," *Journal of Finance* (June 1978), Vol. 33, No. 3, pp. 903-16.

Fuller, Russel J., and Metcalf, Richard W. "Management Disclosures: Analysts Prefer Facts to Management's Predictions," *Financial Analysts Journal* (March/April 1978), Vol. 34, No. 2, pp. 55-57.

Garrett, Ray, Jr. "The Role of Financial Public Relations." Address presented to the Publicity Club of Chicago, March 13, 1974, Chicago, Ill., p. 3.

Gillis, John. "Securities Law and Corporate Disclosure," *Public Relations Journal* (April 1976), Vol. 32, No. 4, pp. 18-21.

Gonodes, Nicholas. "A Note on Accounting-Based and Market-Based Estimates of Systematic Risk," *Journal of Financial and Quantitative Analysis* (June 1975), Vol. 10, No. 2, pp. 355-66.

——————. Session Topic: Finance and Accounting. "The Capital Market, The Market for Information, and External Accounting," *Journal of Finance* (May 1976), Vol. 31, No. 2, pp. 611-30.

Gooding, Arthur E. "Perceived Risk and Capital Asset Pricing," *Journal of Finance* (December 1978), Vol. 33, No. 5, pp. 1401-24.

Gordon, Myron J. "The Savings, Investment and Valuation of a Corporation," *Review of Economics and Statistics* (February 1962), Vol. 44, No. 1, pp. 37-51.

Graham, Benjamin, Dodd, David L., and Cottle, Sidney. *Security Analysis: Principles and Technique,* 4th edition. New York: McGraw-Hill, 1962, p. 711.

Granger, Clive W. J., and Morgenstern, Oskar. "Spectral Analysis of New York Stock Market Prices," *Kyklos* (1963), Vol. 16, pp. 1-27.

Griffin, Paul A. "Competivive Information in the Stock Market: An Empirical Study of Earnings, Dividends and Analysts Forecasts," *Journal of Finance* (May 1976), Vol. 31, No. 2, pp. 631-50.

Horwitz, B. and Kolodny, R. "Line of Business Reporting and Security Prices: An Analysis of an SEC Disclosure Rule," *Bell Journal of Economics and Management Science* (Spring 1977), Vol. 8, No. 1, pp. 234-49.

Hagerman, Robert L., and Richmond, Richard D. "Random Walks, Martingales and the OTC," *Journal of Finance* (September 1973), Vol. 28, No. 4, pp. 897-909.

Hamburger, M. J., and Kochin, L. A. "Money and Stock Prices: The Channels of Influence," *Journal of Finance* (May 1972), Vol. 27, No. 2, pp. 231-49.

Haugen, Richard A., and Wichern, Dean W. "The Diametric Effects of the Captial Gains Tax on the Stability of Security Prices," *Journal of Finance* (September 1973), Vol. 28, No. 4, pp. 987-96.

Hendershott, Patrick H., and Van Horne, James C. "Expected Inflation Implied by Captial Rates," *Journal of Finance* (May 1973), Vol. 28, No. 2, pp. 301-14.

Holmes, John Russel. "100 Years of Common Stock Investing," *Financial Analysts Journal* (November/December 1974), Vol. 30, No. 6, pp. 38-44.

Homa, Kenneth E., and Jaffe, Dwight. "The Supply of Money and Common Stock Prices," *Journal of Finance* (December 1971), Vol. 26, No. 5, pp. 1045-66.

Ibbotson, Roger G. "Price Performance of Common Stock New Issues," *Journal of Financial Economics* (May 1975), Vol. 2, No. 1.

_____., and Jaffe, Jeffery F. "'Hot Issue' Markets," *Journal of Finance* (September 1975), Vol. 30, No. 4, pp. 1027-42.

The Institute of Chartered Financial Analysts. *Fifteenth Directory of Members, 1977-78.* Charlottesville, Va.: ICFA, 1978.

The Institute of Chartered Financial Analysts, 1979-1980 Supplement to 1977-1978 Membership Directory. Charlottesville, Va.: ICFA, 1979.

Jacob, Nancy. "The Measurement of Systematic Risk for Securities and Portfolios: Some Empirical Evidence," *Journal of Financial and Quantitative Analysis* (March 1971), Vol. 6, No. 2, pp. 815-34.

Jaffe, Jeffery F. "Special Information and Insider Trading," *Journal of Business* (July, 1974), Vol. 47, No. 3, pp. 410-28.

_____., and Winkler, Robert L. "Optimal Speculation Against an Efficient Market," *Journal of Finance* (March 1976), Vol. 31, No. 1, pp. 49-61.

Jen, Frank C. "Discussion," *Journal of Finance* (May 1970), Vol. 25, No. 2, pp. 495-99.

Jensen, Michael C. "Capital Markets: Theory and Evidence," *The Bell Journal of Economics and Management Science* (Autumn 1972), Vol. 3, No. 2, pp. 167-247.

_____. "The Performance of Mutual Funds in the Period 1945-64," *Journal of Finance* (May 1968), Vol. 23, No. 2, pp. 389-416.

_____. "Risk, The Pricing of Capital Assets, and the Evaluation of Investment Portfolios," *Journal of Business* (April 1969), Vol. 42, No. 2, pp. 167-247.

_____., and Bennington, George A. "Random Walks and Technical Theories: Some Additional Evidence," *Journal of Finance* (May 1970), Vol. XXV, No. 2, pp. 460-82.

Johnson, Glenn L., Reilly, Frank K., and Smith, Ralph E. "Individual Common Stocks as Inflation Hedges," *Journal of Financial and Quantitative Analysis* (June 1971), Vol. 6, No. 3, pp.1015-24.

Jordan, Ronald J. "An Empirical Investigation of the Adjustment of Stock Prices to New Quarterly Earnings Information," *Journal of Financial and Quantitative Analysis* September 1973), Vol. 8, No. 4, pp. 609-20.

Joselyn, Robert W. *Designing the Marketing Research Project.* Lexington, N.Y.: Petrocelli/ Charter, Inc., 1977, p. 140.

Kahn, Irving. "Lemmings Always Lose," *Financial Analysts Journal* (May/June 1977), Vol. 33, No. 3, pp. 27-30.

Kaplan, R. and Roll, R. W. "Accounting Changes and Stock Prices," *Financial Analysts Journal* (January/February 1973), Vol. 29, No. 1, pp. 48-53.

Kapnick, Harvey E. "Will Financial Forecasts Really Help Investors?" *Financial Executive* (August 1972), Vol. 40, No. 8, pp. 50-54.

Kendall, Maurice G. "The Analysis of Economic Time-Series—Part I: Prices," *Journal of the Royal Statistical Society* (1953), Vol. 96, Pt. I, pp. 11-25.

Kennedy, Robert E. Instructional Notes, Portfolio Management Class, University of Arkansas.

Kruizenga, Richard J. "Profit Returns from Purchasing Puts and Calls," *Random Character of Stock Market Prices.* Cambridge, Mass.: MIT Press, pp. 392-411.

Kuehner, Charles D. "Efficient Markets and Random Walk," *Financial Analysts Handbook,* Vol. 1. Homewood, Ill.: Dow-Jones-Irwin, 1975.

Laffer, Arthur B. "Do Investors Need More Information?" *The Attack on Corporate America.* New York: McGraw-Hill, 1978, pp. 109-10.

Laporte, Lowell. *Investor Relations.* Studies in Business Policy, No. 124. New York: National Industrial Conference Board, 1967.

Latane, Henry A., and Young, William E. "Test of Portfolio Building Rules," *Journal of Finance* (September 1969), Vol. 24, No. 4, pp. 595-612.

Levy, Haim, and Sarnat, Marshall. "The Case for Mutual Funds," *Financial Analysts Journal* March-April 1972, Vol. 28, No. 2, pp. 77-81.

Levy, Robert A. "Beta as a Predictor of Return," *Financial Analysts Journal* (January-February 1974), Vol. 30, No. 1, pp. 61-69.

_____. "Conceptual Foundations of Technical Analysis," *Financial Analysts Journal* (July-August, 1966), Vol. 22, No. 4, pp. 83-90.

_____. "On the Short Term Stationarity of Beta Coefficients," *Financial Analysts Journal*

(November/December 1971), Vol. 27, No. 6, pp. 55-62.

———— . "Random Walks: Reality or Myth," *Financial Analysts Journal* (November/ December 1967), Vol. 23, No. 6, pp. 69-76.

———— . "Random Walks: Reality or Myth—Reply," *Financial Analysts Journal* (January/February 1968), Vol. 24, No. 1, pp. 129-32.

Lintner, John. "Presidential Address: Inflation and Security Returns," *Journal of Finance* (May 1975), Vol. 30, No. 2, pp. 259-80.

———— . "Security Prices, Risk, and Maximal Gains From Diversification," *Journal of Finance* (December 1965), Vol. 20, No. 5, pp. 587-616.

———— . "The Valuation of Risk Assets and the Selection of Risky Investments in Stock Portfolios and Capital Budgets," *Review of Economics and Statistics* (February 1965), Vol. 47, No. 1, pp. 13-37.

Logue, Dennis E. "Market-Making and the Assessment of Market Efficiency," *Journal of Finance* (March 1975), Vol. 30, No. 1, pp. 115-23.

———— . "On the Pricing of Unseasoned Equity Issues: 1965-1969," *Journal of Financial and Quantitative Analysis* (January 1973), Vol. 8, No. 1, pp. 91-104.

Lorie, James H., and Hamilton, Mary T., *The Stock Market—Theories and Evidence.* Homewood, Ill.: Richard D. Irwin, Inc., 1973, p. 81.

Lurie, Arlene J., and Pastena, Victor S. "How Promptly Do Corporations Disclose Their Problems?" *Financial Analysts Journal* (September/October 1975), Vol. 31, No. 5, pp. 55-61.

McDonald, John G. "Objectives and Performance of Mutual Funds," *Journal of Financial and Quantitiative Analysis* (June 1974), Vol. 9, No. 3, pp. 311-34.

McKee, James W., and Hindenach, Lee P. "The Corporation and ERISA: For Now and for the Future," *Financial Executive* (June 1975), Vol. 43, No. 6, pp. 16-22.

Mandelbrot, Benoit. "Forecasts of Future Prices, Unbiased Markets, and Martingale Models," *Journal of Business* (Special Supplement) (January 1966), (Vol. 39, No. 1, pp. 242-55.

———— . "The Variation of Certain Speculative Prices," *Journal of Business* (October 1963), Vol. 36, No. 4, pp. 394-419.

Mao, James C. T. "Essentials of Portfolio Diversification Strategy," *Journal of Finance* (December 1970), Vol. 25, No. 5, pp. 1109-21.

Marcus, Bruce W. *Competing for Capital—A Financial Relations Approach.* New York: John Wiley and Sons, 1975.

Markowitz, Harry M. "Markowitz Revisited," *Financial Analysts Journal* (September/ October 1976), Vol. 32, No. 5, pp. 47-52.

———— . "Portfolio Selection," *Journal of Finance* (March 1952), Vol. 7, No. 1, pp. 77-91.

———— . Portfolio Selection. *Cowles Foundation Monograph. New Haven, Ct.: Yale University* Press, 1967.

———— . Portfolio Selection: Efficient Diversification of Investments. New York: John Wiley, 159, p.3.

Marting, Elizabeth, ed. *A Company Guide to Effective Stockholder Relations, with Sections on the Role of the Security Analyst and the Impact of Federal Law.* New York: American Management Association, 1953.

Miller, Edward M. "Risk, Uncertainty, and Divergence of Opinion," *Journal of Finance* (September 1977), Vol. 32, No. 4, pp. 1151-68.

Miller, Merton H., and Modigliani, Franco. "Dividend Policy, Growth, and the Valuation of Shares," *Journal of Business* (October 1961), Vol. 34, No. 4, pp. 411-33.

———— ., and Scholes, Myron S. "Rates of Return in Relation to Risk: A Reexamination of Recent Findings," in *Studies in the Theory of Capital Markets.* New York: Praeger Publishers, Inc., 1972, pp. 47-48. Quoted by Franco Modigliani and Gerald A. Pogue, "An Introduction to Risk and Return: Concepts and Evidence," *Financial Analysts Handbook,* Vol. 1 Homewood, Ill.: Dow Jones-Irwin, 1975, pp. 1330-31.

Miller, Paul F., Jr. *Institutional Service Report—Monthly Review,* Philadelphia: Drexel and Co., Inc., November, 1965.

Modigliani, Franco, and Pogue, Gerald R. "An Introduction to Risk and Return: Concepts and Evidence," *Financial Analysts Handbook,* Vol. 1. Homewood, Ill.: Dow Jones-Irwin, 1975, pp. 1135-36.

————. , and Pogue, Gerald R. "An Introduction to Risk and Return–II," *Financial Analysts Journal* (May/June 1974), Vol. 30, No. 3, pp. 69-85.

————. , and Miller, Merton H. "Corporate Income Tax as the Cost of Capital: A Correction," *American Economic Review* (June 1963), Vol. 13, No. 3, pp. 433-43.

Morrison, Russell J. "Musings of a Portfolio Manager," *Financial Analysts Journal* (May/June 1975), Vol. 31, No. 3, pp. 37-41.

Mossin, Jan, "Equilibrium in a Capital Asset Market," *Econometrica* (October 1966), Vol. 34, No. 4, pp. 768-83.

National Investor Relations Institute. *A Broad-Based Study of the Investor Relations Professional.* Washington, D.C.: NIRI, 1974.

National Investor Relations Institute. A Perspective on Investor Relations. Washington, D.C.: NIRI, 1979.

————. *Membership Directory, 1978.* Washington, D.C.: NIRI, 1978.

Neiderhoffer, Victor, and Regan, Patrick J. "Earnings Changes, Analysts Forecasts and Stock Prices," *Financial Analysts Journal* (May/June 1972), Vol. 28, No. 3, pp. 65-72.

Norby, William C. "Overview of Financial Analysis," *Financial Analysts Handbook.* Homewood, Ill.: Dow Jones-Irwin, 1975.

————. , and Stone, Frances G. "Objectives of Financial Accounting and Reporting from the Viewpoint of the Financial Analysts," *Financial Analysts Journal* (July/August 1972), Vol. 28, No. 4, pp. 39-45/76-81.

NYSSA Round Table. "The Outlook for Security Analysts," *Financial Analysts Journal* (November/December 1973), Vol. 29, No. 6, pp. 22-29.

Osborne, M.F.M. "Brownian Motion in the Stock Market," *Operations Research* (March/April 1959), Vol. 7, No. 2, pp. 145-73.

Peake, Junius W. "The National Market System," *Financial Analysts Journal* (July/August 1978), Vol. 34, No. 4, pp. 25-34.

Pettit, R. Richardson and Westerfield, Randolph. "Using the Capital Asset Pricing Model and the Market Model to Predict Security Returns," *Journal of Financial and Quantitative Analysis* (September 1974), Vol. 9, No. 4, pp. 579-606.

Phillippatos, George C., and Nawrocki, David N. "The Information Inaccuracy of Stock Market Forecasts: Some New Evidence on Dependence on the New York Stock Exchange," *Journal of Financial and Quantitative Analysis* (June 1973), Vol. 8, No. 3, pp. 445-58.

Pinches, George E. "The Random Walk and Technical Analysis," *Financial Analysts Journal* (March/April 1970), Vol. 26, No. 2, pp. 104-09.

————. , and Singleton, J. Clay. "Earnings Changes, Stock Prices, and Market Efficiency," *Journal of Finance* (March 1978), Vol. 33, No. 1, pp. 29-44.

Reilly, Frank K., Smith, Ralph E., and Johnson, Glenn L. "A Correction and Update Regarding Individual Common Stocks as Inflation Hedges," *Journal of Financial and Quantitative Analysis* (December 1975), Vol. 10, No. 5, pp. 871-80.

————. , and William C. Slaughter. "The Effect of Dual Markets on Common Stock Market Making," *Journal of Financial and Quantitative Analysis* (March 1973), Vol. 8, No. 2, pp. 167-82.

Report of the Advisory Committee on Corporate Disclosure to the SEC. Washington, D.C.: Government Printing Office, 1976.

Robbins, H. Zane. "Your New Quarterly Report," *Public Relations Journal* (April 1976), Vol. 32, No. 4, pp. 24-26.

Roberts, Harry V. "Stock Market Patterns and Financial Analysis: Methodological Suggestions," *Journal of Finance* (March 1959), Vol. 14, No. 1, pp. 1-10.

Robichek, Alexander A. "Risk and the Value of Securities," *Journal of Financial and Quantitative Analysis* (December 1969), Vol. 4, No. 4, pp. 513-38.

Robinson, Edward J. *Public Relations and Survey Research.* New York: Meredith Corporation, 1969.

Rosenberg, Barr. "Extra-Market Components of Covariance in Security Returns," *Journal of Financial and Quantitative Analysis* (March 1974), Vol. 9, No. 2, pp. 263-74.

————. , and McKibben, Walt. "The Prediction of Systematic and Specific Risk in Common

Stocks," *Journal of Financial and Quantitative Analysis* (March 1973), Vol. 8, No. 2, pp. 317-34.

Ross, Stephen. "The Current Status of the CAPM," *Journal of Finance* (June 1978), Vol. 33, No. 3, pp. 885-902.

Rozeff, Michael S. "The Money Supply and the Stock Market," *Financial Analysts Journal* (September/October 1975), Vol. 31, No. 5, pp. 18-27.

Rudolph, J. Allan. "Stock Prices and the Money Supply," *Financial Analysts Journal* (March/April 1972), Vol. 28, No. 2, pp. 19-26.

Samuelson, P.A. "Proof That Properly Discounted Present Values of Assets Vibrate Randomly," *Bell Journal of Economics and Management Science* (Autumn 1973), Vol. 4, No. 2, pp. 369-74.

Schlarbaum, Gary G., Lewellen, Wilbur G., and Lease, Ronald C. "The Common Stock—Portfolio Performance Records of Individual Investors: 1964-70," *Journal of Finance* (May 1978), Vol. 33, No. 2, pp. 429-42.

Scholes, Myron. "The Market for Securities: Substitution Versus Price Pressure and the Effects of Information on Share Prices," *Journal of Business* (April 1972), Vol. 45, No. 2, pp. 179-211.

"Second Thoughts About the "Efficient Market" in "A Difference of Opinion," an interview of William F. Sharpe and J. Michael Murphy by A.F. Ehrbar, *Fortune* (February 26, 1979), Vol. 99, No. 4, pp. 105-07.

Shapiro, Alan C. "Exchange Rate Changes, Inflation, and the Value of the Multinational Corporation," *Journal of Finance* (May 1975), Vol. 30, No. 2, pp. 485-502.

Sharma, J.L., and Kennedy, Robert E. "A Comparative Analaysis of Stock Price Behavior on the Bombay, London, and New York Stock Exchanges," *Journal of Financial and Quantitative Analysis* (September 1977), Vol. 12, No. 3, pp. 391-413.

Sharpe, William F. "Bonds vs. Stocks: Capital Market Theory," *Financial Analysts Journal* (November/December 1973), Vol. 29, No. 6, pp. 74-80.

_____ . "Diversification and Portfolio Risk," *Financial Analysts Journal* (January-February, 1972), Vol. 28, No. 1, pp. 74-79.

_____ . "Inputing Expected Security Returns from Portfolio Composition," *Journal of Financial and Quantitative Analysis* (June 1974), Vol. 9, No. 3, pp. 463-72.

_____ . *Investments*. Englewood Cliffs, N.J.: Prentice-Hall, Inc., 1978, p. 118.

_____ . *Portfolio Theory and Capital Markets*. New York: McGraw-Hill, 1970, pp. 118-22.

_____ . , and G.M. Cooper. "NYSE Stocks Classified by Risk, 1931-1967," *Financial Analysts Journal* (March/April 1972), Vol. 28, No. 2, pp. 46-55.

Shiskin, Julius. "Systematic Aspects of Stock Price Fluctuations," University of Chicago, Seminar on the Analysis of Security Prices, May, 1968.

Siegel, Jeremy J., and Warner, Harold B. "Indexation, the Risk-Free Asset, and Capital Market Equilibrium," *Journal of Finance* (September 1977), Vol. 32, No. 4, pp. 1101-07.

Siegel, Sidney. *Non-Parametric Statistics for the Behavioral Sciences*. New York: McGraw-Hill, 1956, pp. 104-11.

Singhvi, Surendra S. "Corporate Management's Inclination to Disclose Financial Information," *Financial Analysts Journal* (July/August 1972), Vol. 28, No. 4, pp. 66-73.

Smith, E.L. *Common Stocks as Long-Term Investments*. New York: The Macmillan Company, 1924.

Snyder, Wayne W. "Horse Racing: Testing the Efficient Markets Model," *Journal of Finance* (September 1978), Vol. 33, No. 4, pp. 1109-18.

Spigelman, Joseph H. "What Basis for Superior Performance?" *Financial Analysts Journal* (May/June 1974), Vol. 30, No. 3, pp. 32-45.

Tabel, Edmund W., and Tabell, Anthony W. "The Case for Technical Analysts," *Financial Analysts Journal* (March/April 1964), Vol. 20, No. 2, pp. 67-76.

Terborgh, George. "Inflation and Profits," *Financial Analysts Journal* (May/June 1974), Vol. 30, No. 3, pp. 19-23.

Umstead, David A. "Forecasting Stock Market Prices," *Journal of Finance* (May 1977), Vol. 32, No. 2, pp. 427-41.

Van Horne, J.C., and Glassmire, W.F. "The Impact of Unanticipated Changes in Inflation on the Value of Common Stocks," *Journal of Finance* (December 1972), Vol. 27, No. 5, pp. 1051-92.

Vasicek, O.A., and McQuown, J.A. "The Efficient Market Model," *Financial Analysts Journal* (September/October 1972), Vol. 28, No. 5, pp. 71-84.

Wagner, W.H., and Zipkin, C.A. "Better Performance via Inventory Funds," *Financial Analysts Journal* (May/June 1978), Vol. 34, No. 3, pp. 34-37.

Wallich, Henry C. "Traditional vs. Performance Stock Valuations," *Commercial and Financial Chronicle* (February 18 1971), Vol. 213, No. 7074, pp. 1-5.

_____ . "What Does the Random Walk Hypothesis Mean to Security Analysts?" *Financial Analysts Journal* (March/April 1968), Vol. 24, No. 2, pp. 159-62.

Weston, J. Fred. *The Scope and Methodology of Finance.* Foundations of Finance Series. Englewood Cliffs, N.J.: Prentice-Hall, Inc., 1966.

Williams, J.B. *The Theory of Investment Value.* Cambridge, Mass.: Harvard University Press, 1938.

Williams, William D. "FAF Corporate Information Committee Awards for Excellence in Corporate Reporting for 1976," *Financial Analysts Journal* (Januay 1978), Vol. 34, No. 1, pp. 42-45.

Williamson, Peter J. "Measuring Mutual Fund Performance," *Financial Analysts Journal* (November-December, 1972), Vol. 28, No. 6, pp. 78-91.

Working, Holbrook. "A Random-Difference Series for Use in the Analysis of Time Series," *Journal of the American Statistical Association* (March 1934), Vol. 29, No. 185, pp. 11-24.

Index